# A Bartender's Guide To Carding

A Guide To Checking ID And Spotting Fakes For The Alcohol And Marijuana Industries

By
**Thomas Morrell**

**UNIFORM23**
TRAINING

## Copyright Notice

## Trademark Disclaimer

## Copyright Acknowledgement

## Legal Disclaimer

## Introduction

Alcohol and marijuana are both intoxicants. They're intoxicants that are sold through a legal regulatory system that is designed to ensure public safety, responsible consumption and professional accountability for vendors.

What does that mean?

In plain speak, that means that alcohol and marijuana get people drunk and high. There are laws about how people can legally get drunk and high. There are also laws about who and how employees and businesses can sell these products. Those laws are designed to keep people safe. That means, both the person consuming the intoxicants, as well as the community at large and the people and businesses that sell these products.

You can't legally drive a car when you're drunk. You can operate a forklift while you're high. You have to be a certain age to legally buy alcohol and marijuana as set by law. If you sell alcohol and marijuana you are required by law to check IDs and verify the age of your customers.

That last one is what this book is all about.

In America, every state regulates how old a person has to be in order to buy alcohol and marijuana. These laws are designed with a variety of goals in mind. Younger people are still developing physically and alcohol and marijuana can affect that development. Also, younger people may lack the proper maturity and decision making abilities to consume these intoxicants in a safe, responsible way.

For whatever reasons these laws were enacted, they're literally the law of the land. Regardless if you are a supervisor or an employee in the alcohol or marijuana industries, it's your job to enforce these laws. If you are a supervisor, it may be your job to design systems that promote compliance as well.

Why is all of this important?

Employees who fail to follow the law, or who are caught in a law enforcement sting can be fined and criminally prosecuted. They (and your business) can even be sued in civil court if their failure to enforce the law results in liability, injury or death. I have personally witnessed high fines and criminal convictions for a failed sting. That employee's life was turned upside down.

Business owners and managers are not exempt either. They can be held liable for the actions of their employees and can likewise be fined, and sued. In a worst case scenario your business can be subject to license restrictions, suspensions or revocations. For many businesses that exist to sell alcohol and marijuana, this is a death sentence for your business, your investment and maybe your nest egg.

These punishments pale in comparison to someone being injured or even dying in a motor vehicle or similar accident. At the end of the day, we are people who live in a community who have to look at ourselves in the mirror. For me, the fear of having someone's injury or death on my conscience is always a powerful motivator to adhere to the law and to conduct myself responsibly.

It's a lot of responsibility. It's a lot of pressure. It's on all of our shoulders.

It is not, however, an impossible task to provide amazing customer service while complying with the law and running a safe business. This book can help you manage that responsibility effectively.

How?

To manage this responsibility effectively a business needs policies and procedures and trained employees. This book will help to establish both regardless of what role you play in your organization.

Think of the policies and procedures as "the plan". The trained employees then execute "the plan". You need both to be successful. If there is no policy, employees won't know what to do in situations they will find themselves in. If they aren't trained, they can't execute the policy.

What if you're an employee and don't have anything to do with policy?

I have always been a firm believer in the idea that the best ideas come from the bottom of an organization. That layer of employees are the ones that have contact with customers and have the most direct experience. They also have the most impact on customer service and driving forward the business' culture.

I am all about empowering these folks. If you are an employee, you may become a supervisor and may need to set a policy at some point. If you are happy as an employee and want to stay one forever, that's fine! But, you still have wisdom and experience and may be able to make suggestions to your supervisors to make things better or more clear.

However you want to slice it, as an employee, having a good idea of what a carding policy should look like will help you, your coworkers, your supervisor and your business.

If you're a manager, you may never have been taught this stuff. You may have a plate that is so overloaded you forget your own name some days. I have been there! I have worked in operations with no manuals, policies or training. It can be rough.

For you, this will show you everything you need to think about to quickly establish basic policies and procedures.

Let's get started!

## Part 1: Establishing Proper Procedures, Policies & Educational Systems

Proper policy sets the tone and drives the culture in the workplace. In this section, I will lay out all the points that should be considered and decided on by management to establish a proper carding procedure. Remember, just because you are not in management does not mean you can't help to establish an effective carding policy. In fact, since you are the customer facing employees and very often have the most amount of experience in carding situations, your input and experience can be invaluable!

**Why An Effective Carding Program Matters To Everyone**

Without a reliable, well administered carding program in place, sooner or later someone will violate the law, be cited, fined, sued or the business you have been entrusted to work at or manager will suffer. You will usually wind up suffering too through fines, loss of income, unemployment or the business closing.

I will give you a case example to show how things can quickly go wrong in these situations.

Some years back, an establishment that I was familiar with did not have an effective carding program in place. They offered slot machine gambing in a section of the establishment, which was legal, but much like liquor and marijuana, is age restricted and requires proper ID for age verification.

Due to the lack of proper carding procedures and a lax workplace culture, a minor was able to access the machines. This fact became known to the state gaming board.

An investigation resulted and the establishment was fined a large amount of money for this gross violation. This proved to be more than the establishment could bear financially and the business closed shortly afterwards. The employees were let go. They were all unemployed and had to find new jobs.

The manager lost their paycheck. The business owner suffered a loss to their investment.

All of this could have been avoided if the employees and owner had just done what was expected and legally of them. This was an unforced error that could have been avoided at several points along the chain of errors.

Let's look at the chain of errors and then we can talk about how to avoid each link.

1. The manager did not create an effective carding policy or training program.
2. The employees were not effectively carding.
3. There was a lack of supervision related to carding
4. There was no ongoing training concerning proper IDing and fake IDs.
5. No records were being kept about ongoing training

The first step in breaking this chain of errors is to create a policy creating expectations for carding.

## Creating An Effective Carding Policy

In the following sections, I'm going to assume that I'm talking to an organization and it's employees that has zero in the way of carding management, training and policy. Trust me, there are many of them out there. I chose this path because it will help to illustrate, for all stakeholders, how to build an effective management system from the ground up. If your organization has some elements of the program I'm going to outline, you may benefit from new ideas or an aspect you haven't considered before. If you work for an organization without a policy, you can follow this plan, step by step to create one. It's a turnkey solution.

Once that is done, you will have a solid foundation to support ongoing training and efficient day to day, legally compliant management and operations.

### Establish A Point Person

Whoever runs the licensed business on a day to day basis is responsible for creating carding policies and seeing to their implementation. If you own the business - great. You're now the point person. If you run the business 100% - great. You're now the point person. If there is more than one hand in the cookie jar, a conversation should be had with all the interested parties and someone should become the point person on carding policies and training.

There are a lot of mom and pop shops out there. I couldn't even begin to tell you how many neighborhood bars and corner taverns there are in America. We can just agree that there are a lot. Many, many of these establishments are run as small family businesses that may have never considered writing a policy manual.

I have spent time in this world and often, management and ownership mix and the chain of command can get convoluted. Who is taking responsibility for things can become unclear or everybody involved in running the place can think that someone else is taking care of a problem. These problems and management chores can then fall through the cracks.

Carding and age verification cannot be one of the things that fall through the cracks. Your business just can't afford it. Start to manage this risk by assigning a point person today!

Call a meeting. Have a sit down. Make a phone call. Do it now, while you're reading this and while it's fresh in your mind.

## Put It In Writing

Once your organization has established a point person for carding, the next step is to put the carding and age verification policy in writing.

You might be thinking that this is a black and white issue. You could forgive someone for assuming something like "Make sure everyone is 21" would be sufficient. It's not, and we will explore why in the following sections.

### Which IDs do we accept?

Everyone who works in the business needs to know which IDs they can accept and which ones they cannot. Let's start with this part of the policy as it will help us build more on later.

Imagine someone comes into your establishment and they offer you a concealed pistol license as proof that they are over 21.

This is identification. It has a picture in many cases. It will list their birthdate. On its face, this ID would appear to be sufficient to prove someone is 21.

There's just one problem. In many cases, a concealed pistol license is issued by a county sheriff. This makes it a county level identification. State liquor and marijuana laws most often require that identification must be a **STATE** issued ID. A county level ID would fall below this threshold. Accepting a county issued concealed pistol license could be a citable offense and could be grounds for failing a compliance sting in many cases. This would result in fines and possible prosecution.

The same would be true for a county jail ID. Again, on its face, this would appear to be sufficient to prove age, but as another county issued ID, it may not meet state legal requirements.

I have encountered these specific situations numerous times in my career. Most likely, sooner or later, everyone who works in a bar will run into them too. They may even run into new ones I have never heard of. When faced with a situation like this, employees need clear guidance on what IDs are acceptable and which ones are not. If that guidance is missing, they may make decisions on the spot that are wrong. Mistakes will be made that can be costly.

These mistakes are 100% avoidable by listing what IDs are acceptable in a comprehensive carding policy.

If I were writing a carding policy, the first thing I would look at is which IDs are acceptable. The place to start is with your state regulatory authority. You have their contact info handy already, because they are the ones who issued your liquor or marijuana license.

Most likely, there is a list, written into official state law that tells you what you can legally accept as proof of age. All others, cannot be accepted.

As a general rule, regulators want you to be successful and to comply with the law. It makes their jobs easier. When you ask questions ahead of time, to prevent problems from developing, they are usually very, very helpful. They often have publications and posters that they will send you to help educate your staff as well - free of charge.

As a first step to your policy, contact your regulators now. Ask them what IDs you can legally accept as proof of age.

The list that you receive from the regulators will be the list of IDs that you **CAN** legally accept. It will be your job as a manager to decide what IDs you **WILL** accept. They do not have to be the same and in many cases, there are good reasons that the list of IDs you will accept should be more restricted than the list of IDs that you can legally accept.

As an example of this concept, let's consider a European driver's license.

These are standardized forms that are used by all 26 members of the European Union. They have the exact same form in Scotland that they do in Latvia that they do in Italy. The only element that changes is the language that the ID is written in. They are always written in the issuing country's official language. They're commonly presented by traveler's and foreign exchange students in bars and restaurants all over America. Patrons and guests have presented them to me countless times.

If you are unfamiliar with this ID type, do a quick Google search for "European Union ID" to see the most current example.

These IDs are official, legal, state issued IDs that present your staff with some challenges. First, they're written in excess of 15 languages. Most of which your employees will not be able to read. State laws can require that, in order to accept an ID, it must be written in a language that the examiner can read. If your employee accepts an ID written in Czech and they can't read Czech, it can be a citable offense. This is true regardless of whether or not you understand what the dates on the ID mean.

In addition, I've seen these IDs cause other problems as well. Because many ID checkers are unfamiliar with them, they may just accept them without any actual examination. ID checkers may not have the resources to verify them (we will talk about these resources later) or they may not be familiar with security and anti-counterfeiting features since they rarely see them. Fake IDs of this type, like many driver's licenses can be easily purchased online as well and can be presented to bouncers and bartenders in bad faith. Their exotic nature only raises the chances that someone will make a mistake and accept one when they shouldn't.

We will talk more about fake IDs later.

The bottom line is that accepting these IDs opens up a lot of security holes that may not be ideal or convenient to your business. You can choose not to accept them and to require someone present their passport instead.

Someone presenting an EU driver's license is most likely visiting the United States. They should have a passport. Passports are much more universal documents, written in English, French and the native language and are much harder to counterfeit. Buying a fake passport online is much harder than buying a fake driver's license. Candidly, international authorities and law enforcement take the issue of counterfeit passports much more seriously than they do a fake Arkansa driver's license. As such, passports offer more assurance that the person is who they say they are and that they are of age.

Choosing to not accept EU driver's licenses (although legally permitted to) and instead requiring a passport is an example of a house policy. A house policy is a more restrictive policy than is legally required that your business chooses to enforce. It's designed to provide a safe, well run business beyond what the law requires.

Another example of a house policy would be saying that a person can be served a maximum of four alcoholic beverages. State law may say otherwise, but your business enforces this policy to help ensure a well run establishment.

The house policies on acceptable IDs should be the first thing you set down in your written policy. Do your due diligence and check with your state regulators.

The following list is an example of what a final list of acceptable IDs might look like:

- Valid passport
- Valid state issued Driver's License
- Valid state issued Identification Card
- Valid United States Military Identification Card
- Foreign driver's licenses are **NOT ACCEPTABLE**
- County issued IDs are **NOT ACCEPTABLE**

Passports, driver's licenses and identification cards are all commonly understood forms of ID. As a general rule, in my experience, I have always accepted passports. Like I said before, they are written in English, French and the official language of the issuing government. They are very hard to fake or to buy counterfeit, so in my opinion, they establish to a high degree of certainty of both identity and age.

As for driver's licenses and ID cards, I have usually limited my policies to the driver's licenses of the fifty United States states, the District of Columbia and the five US territories. These are Guam, Puerto Rico, American Samoa, The US Virgin Islands and the Northern Mariana Islands. I have personally seen all of these IDs at one point or another, including all of the territories.

I have usually not accepted foreign driver's licenses for the same reasons we talked about with the EU driver's license. They create risks and challenges that are difficult to manage with certainty. This may require that you have a candid conversation with a potential customer to explain why you have made this decision. Although they are often frustrated with the refusal, I have found more often than not that explaining the matter politely, patiently and understandingly will go a long way. I would usually end those interactions by inviting them back with their passport. If things were particularly tense, I found that offering to buy them a drink or appetizer on their return visit would leave most people satisfied. Both employees and managers may be tasked with having these challenging conversations, so it's not a bad idea to think about how they might best be handled ahead of time.

What about military IDs and federally issued IDs? It's possible to go a whole career and not run into them. Let's spend some time making sure you're familiar with these so you can teach your employees.

Military identification cards are IDs that are issued by the United States Department of Defense. There are two types of IDs issued by the Department of Defense. The first is issued to enlisted military personnel of all five U.S. military branches. These are the Army, Navy, Air Force, Marine Corps and the Coast Guard. Reservists and ROTC cadets (present at most colleges) will also be issued these IDs.

These IDs can also be issued to civilian contractors of the military and will have a similar form. The fact that they are a civilian contractor will be noted on the ID.

The other type of ID that is issued by the Defense Department is a Uniformed Services Card. This ID is issued to members of military families as well as retired military personnel.

Because both types of ID issued by the Defense Department are issued by the federal government, they are higher security IDs than state issued IDs like driver's licenses. They are more on par with passports and as a general rule, have always been sufficient ID in my professional experience.

To see the most current, as well as previous versions of the current IDs issued by the United States military visit **www.cac.mil** . I am not familiar with military IDs of any other nation. I have also, as far as I can recall, never been presented with one in an attempt to prove age. Needless to say, I would not accept those or recommend to anyone reading this to accept those.

What about federally issued identification cards, not issued by the Department of Defense? There are 15 other executive departments that are not the Department of Defense. That means that there are many different IDs. Every park ranger, labor investigator, FBI agent, federal prison guard and customs officer is issued an ID. They are constantly changing and evolving as security features are added and new designs are introduced. This means there is no hard and fast rule and I cannot offer you examples of every ID out there.

I can also say that most of the time, these IDs are not offered as proof of age in a business that offers alcohol or marijuana. I can think of only one instance where this has come up in my career and as I'm getting older, I can't even recall the department. As with everything else, check with your local regulators to see what the current law is and what is allowed before you write anything down in your policy.

The federally issued IDs that do come up from time to time are Merchant Mariner Credential documents and immigration documents like Residency Permits and Green Cards. Let's briefly talk about those.

Let's start with the Merchant Mariner Credential IDs. The Merchant Mariner Credential (MMC) is a type of ID that is issued by the United States Coast Guard to personnel involved in the shipping industry. It's very similar in appearance to a passport, and for transportation workers, serves the same function at ports overseas. The major difference between an MMC and a passport is that the cover of the MMC is red, while US passports are blue. It's an official, federally issued ID and contains much of the same info as a passport. At one point in my career, I worked very close to a busy port and these showed up in the restaurant periodically.

For the most current info on MMCs and to see the current design visit **www.dco.uscg.mil/nmc/merchant_Marinerr_credential/** .

The US Department of Homeland Security issues many different documents to foreigners who have been granted rights in the United States. These may be as simple as a visa document for a temporary, longer term visit. They may be a work permit that allows the bearer to legally work in the United States. They may also be a permanent resident card (often called a green card) to reside in the United States indefinitely.

I have been presented all of these documents as proof of age in my time in the hospitality industry and as a matter of practice, I have always accepted these as valid, federally issued IDs. Work permits and green cards are usually cards that are similar to a driver's license in appearance. Visas are usually a sticker that is fixed inside a valid passport. People visiting the US on a long term visa will be used to presenting them as ID and often will offer that page instead of the passport's ID section.

For the most current for of IDs issued by the Department of Homeland Security you can visit their website at www.uscis.gov/i-9-central/form-i-9-resources/handbook-for-employers-m-274/120-acceptable-documents-for-verifying-employment-authorization-and-identity/121-list-a-documents-that-establish-identity-and-employment-authorization . (Sorry that one is so long.)

There are two other types of IDs that I feel pressed to talk about as they have both been presented to me in my career and may create challenges for your employees.

These are Consular IDs and Native American Tribal IDs. Both can be sensitive subjects and should be handled respectfully and professionally. To do that, you need to know what they are and what the law permits and requires where you operate.

First, what are these?

Consular IDs are ID cards that are issued by foreign embassies in the United States to use as IDs while foreign citizens are in the US. These are generally issued regardless of immigration status and are designed to help the citizens of the issuing country while they reside in the United States. It is possible that the bearer of a consular ID does not have a passport. The two forms I have personally seen in my time are the Mexican and Guatemalan versions.

As of the writing of this work, in my state, to my knowledge, consular IDs are not legally acceptable IDs as proof of age or identity. Before determining how these IDs fit into your written policy, you should consult your state regulator for the most current information.

Native American tribal IDs are IDs that are issued by the tribal governments of Native American nations inside the US. They serve as ID for the citizens of these nations. I have been presented this type of ID only two times in my career. However, depending on where you live and operate, you may have a different experience. The largest Native American nation in the United States has almost 200,000 citizens.

Native American reservations are federally recognized jurisdictions, and as such, their members are United States citizens. The reservations are not state level entities and have a special status that is similar to United States territories. They are part of the US and when residents move between the reservation and other non-reservation US jurisdictions, they are doing so as US citizens the whole time. As such, they do not need a passport. It is very possible that they will not have one with them (they don't need it) and they may not have one at all.

When I first started bartending, Native American IDs were not written into law as acceptable ID forms. This prevented me from accepting them by law. However, fortunately, in the state where I reside, the law has finally caught up and these IDs were recently added to the list of acceptable IDs. Before you decide on these IDs as part of your written policy, an inquiry should be made to your regulators.

That's going to bring our discussion of ID types to a close.

There are a lot of IDs out there as you may have just learned; and it gets more complicated every time a state issues a new ID format. IDs change, laws change and, unfortunately, every responsible employee needs to keep up on all of this. It's a pain, but it's necessary, important work.

As you read through this section, you may have noticed a theme. I kept encouraging you to check with your local regulators and licensing authority. That wasn't an accident and it wasn't me passing the buck. It was me encouraging you to create open and reliable channels of communication with the people who are responsible for setting and enforcing the law on these issues.

I am not a lawyer. I am not providing you with legal advice. You, and you alone are responsible for finding the information you need and for acting within the law. Laws change and policies change, often without your knowledge. It's up to you to ask. You will also be presented with new and unique challenges constantly. Knowing who to talk to, what to ask and how to do it ahead of time will save you time and trouble in the future.

Let's move on to who needs to get carded in your establishment.

**Who Gets Carded?**

At this point, you have a basic understanding of the IDs you might encounter and maybe what should be in a carding policy. If you have any questions or if anything is unclear where you operate, you have an idea of how to find out specifics to make well informed management decisions.

You have an idea what IDs you will accept, but who gets asked for ID in the first place?
This is another idea that needs to be spelled out very clearly in any policy.

Let's start with the "floor".

The floor of your policy is the minimum age of a carding policy. Anyone who looks under this age automatically gets carded.

Often, the minimum carding age will be spelled out in law. You need to check first and make sure you are in compliance with this. Where I live, the floor is 26, by law. Anyone who walks into my business, who looks under 26, must be carded by law. Failure to comply with this is a citable offense.

Whatever your jurisdiction requires is the **legal** carding foor. Remember that we can set more restrictive policies to make sure our businesses are well run, orderly, safe and successful. In many cases, this may mean your policy builds in a margin of error. For example, I have worked for businesses that required anyone who appeared under 30 was carded automatically.

Why would a business do this?

Human error. Pure and simple. Nobody is perfect and nobody gets it right 100% of the time. I have been working in the hospitality industry for more than twenty years and I am still surprised by how old people are. People I think are 25 are 40! It happens. It happens all the time. Nobody is perfect at guessing age.

By setting up a consistent, automatic carding floor, you take the guesswork out of the process and greatly reduce the risk that someone will get through your safeguards.

Why not just card everyone? That way, there won't be any errors or oversights.

This is a delicate subject and to answer this, I am going to lean on my decades of experience.

Carding 100% or your customers will ensure you are in compliance with the law 100% of the time.

If you are running a corner market and you exist and thrive because of location and convenience, this might be a really good way to make sure your employees comply with the law. It will also ensure you avoid fines and management headaches.

This would absolutely be the case for retail marijuana outlets. By all means, park a competent ID checker at the door and make sure they carefully and properly inspect the ID of everyone who comes into your store.

A nightclub would be another venue where I would say that 100% carding is appropriate. Lots of people will try to get in, especially if you have shows. These are busy, happening places and the risk of a slip up is high. Station a bouncer at the front door, card everyone then stamp or bracelet them for good measure.

However, if your business thrives on customer service and hospitality, you may run into some challenges and headaches of your own making. This would be true for restaurants, bars and hotels.

I'll give you an example for you to consider.

Imagine you manage one of these businesses. Imagine you are in the back office and you are writing the schedule for next week. One of your servers comes to you and says there's a problem with the birthday party table. She carded the birthday boy and he doesn't have his ID. She won't serve him and she wants you to talk to them and to back her up.

Your policy requires 100% carding and she was following policy. You should back her up in this situation. So you go to the table.

Right away, you see why the customers are frustrated. It's grandpa's 80th birthday. It's plain as day he's of age. He's been alive longer than you and the waitress put together. However, he didn't bring his ID. He left his wallet at home. It's his party and he wasn't expecting to pay the bill. He doesn't have ID and you have a problem.

In your state, anyone consuming alcohol has to have ID. This guy doesn't have it, doesn't understand the law and doesn't care what your policy is. You're the one ruining his party. He's got every right to be frustrated. You cannot legally serve him in this situation, there's nothing you can do about it, and everyone at that table will leave remembering how your restaurant ruined grandpa's 80th birthday.

This type of situation will come up frequently in a bar or restaurant where there is 100% carding. If it's in a hotel, guests will leave their IDs in the room and will be mad when you make them go get it.

I can tell you with professional certainty that most brides in their wedding dress do not have their ID on them. Their ID is usually back with their street clothes in the hotel room. However, they're not worried about that when they get to the reception and they ask one of your servers for a drink. Telling them no in that situation is particularly upsetting.

In the age of online reviews and social media, managing customer perceptions is a necessary skill to growing your successful business. Sidestepping problems and defusing them before they become an issue is the first place to start when managing your online reputation.

Sidestep the ones I just described by setting a reasonable floor. For me, in my opinion, carding anyone who looks under 35 is very reasonable and sets a big enough buffer zone for any bad age judges on your team.

We have a floor. What about a ceiling?

This one is a lot easier.

As a general rule, I would empower your staff to card anyone, at any time, for any reason. You should make sure they know this. There are many situations, too many to list, where it may be necessary and in the interests of your business to request ID from a guest. It's best not to tie anyone's hands by imposing an artificial ceiling.

At the end of the day, every member of your team needs to feel comfortable and empowered to ask for anyone's ID they feel is necessary, while at the same time knowing that they are required to card anyone who looks (as an example) under 35.

**Manager Open Door Policy**

Managers of any business are better trained, (and hopefully) more experienced leaders. They are empowered to make decisions that other employees cannot or lack the experience and training to make. They are valuable assets to the business and are valuable resources for employees to lean on, utilize and to rely on.

As part of your policy, and any I have ever written, I always advocate for adding a line or two about asking a manager for help.

As a rule, it is never a happy shop or a successful business when employees are afraid to ask their manager questions. I have worked in these places. They absolutely exist. Don't be one of them.

As an employee, you want and need the support of your manager. You will run into weird situations and need a reality check. Angry customers will often ask to speak to your manager and you need to be able to "pass them to the next level". That support is absolutely essential to your success.

As a manager, you want your employees to feel empowered to come to you if they run into something that is unclear or they are unsure of. You want them to check with you so you can help them follow the law, comply with policy and grow as professionals all at once.

I can think of a situation where a server came to me with an ID. They said that the person they had carded only had a foreign ID and didn't have a passport. They were inclined to refuse service. I asked to see the ID.

It was a driver's license from Guam. Guam, as we know, is part of the United States. My server at the time was unaware of this. I took a quick second to explain the situation. My server learned some new stuff, we took care of the customer, adhered to the law and policy all at once.

If my server had been afraid to come to me, it might have ended differently.

When you roll out your policy, however you do it, I would encourage you to make a big deal on this point. Stress that you are there to help. Add that you will work together as a team, to tackle these issues and that there are no stupid questions.

It may sound cheesy, but it's right. It sets the right tone and it helps to build a better, more educated, competent staff in the long run.

**Consequences Of Failing To Follow The Policy**

As a final element to any carding policy, I would suggest a few words about what happens when an employee fails to follow the policy. If you have a policy manual already, this will only reinforce the discipline section. If not, this will establish that this policy is a serious one that should not be taken lightly.

It's best if everyone involved, knows up front that failing on this point will be bad.

Now, again, I am not a lawyer. However, I would advise you to consult with one anytime you change your policy manual or before you present your employees with a new policy. Labor laws and employee relations are complicated parts of the law. Words matter and mistakes can be costly. Much like with what IDs are acceptable, it's better to ask questions before you make a mistake.

**Carding Policy Foundation Examples**

We have done a lot of work up to this point.

We have discussed who will be carded in your business and what IDs you can and should accept. These two concepts will form the foundation of your carding policy. In the next two chapters, we will talk about the last part. That is, how to examine IDs properly and how to spot fake IDs.

At this point, I would encourage you to begin writing your house carding policy. The information is fresh in your head and setting it down now will help you to organize your thoughts.

To help with this, I am providing two samples of carding policies to help you.

It's important that you understand that these are only examples and that you should not use these verbatim. Instead, you should compile your own policy by doing your due diligence, seek competent legal and regulatory advice and counsel, and tailor something specific to your situation.

It's also important that you keep it simple. The longer a policy, the less likely people will be to read it and to understand it. Simple is a virtue with policies. You want a policy that is concise, easily digested, and can fit into an 8"x11" frame for display purposes.

The first policy might be suitable for a retail marijuana store. It will be written with the idea of 100% carding in mind.

## Example #1 - 100% Carding

Anywhere Marijuana Company is committed to selling controlled substances in a responsible way and is committed to being a good corporate citizen. Employees are required to follow this cardng policy for any and all sales of controlled substances.

1. Employees are required to maintain current service permits if required by regulators.

2. Anywhere Marijuana Company requires our employees to require identification that establishes the legal age of all customers seeking to purchase controlled substances.

3. The only forms of identification that can be accepted at Anywhere Marijuana Company are as follows:

- o Valid passport
- o Valid U.S. state issued Driver's License
- o Valid U.S. state issued Identification Card
- o Valid U.S. Military Identification Card
- o Valid federally recognized Native American Tribal ID

4.      The following IDs are **NOT ACCEPTABLE:**

- o   Foreign driver's licenses are **NOT ACCEPTABLE**
- o   County issued IDs are **NOT ACCEPTABLE**

5.      Employees are required to politely refuse the sale of any controlled substance to any      customer who cannot provide satisfactory ID or if the validity of the ID is in doubt.

6.      Employees are required to follow these house policies at all times.  Failure to do so will result in discipline up to and including termination.

## Example #2 - Less Than 100% Carding

Anywhere Restaurants Company is committed to selling alcohol in a responsible way and is committed to being a good corporate citizen. Employees are required to follow this alcohol sales policy for any and all controlled substance sales.

7.      Employees are required to maintain current service permits if required by regulators.

8.      Anywhere Restaurants Company requires our employees to require identification that establishes the legal age of **ALL** customers seeking to purchase controlled substances **WHO APPEAR UNDER 30 YEARS OF AGE**.

9.      The only forms of identification that can be accepted for the sale controlled substances at Anywhere Restaurants Company are as follows:

- o   Valid passport

- Valid U.S. state issued Driver's License
- Valid U.S. state issued Identification Card
- Valid U.S. Military Identification Card
- Valid federally recognized Native American Tribal ID

**10.**    The following IDs are **NOT ACCEPTABLE:**

- Foreign driver's licenses are **NOT ACCEPTABLE**
- County issued IDs are **NOT ACCEPTABLE**

**11.**    Employees are required to politely refuse the sale of alcohol and tobacco to any          customer who cannot provide satisfactory ID or if the validity of the ID is in doubt.

**12.**    Employees are required to follow these house policies at all times. Failure to do so will result in discipline up to and including termination.

**Ongoing Training**

Once you have a policy clearly planned out and documented, it's up to the manager to effectively communicate, explain and teach it to staff. A plan that nobody knows about is useless to everybody.

The first step I would recommend taking is to give everybody a copy of the new policy, in writing. Give them a chance to read it, study it, understand it and ask questions. Consider calling a staff meeting to explain the policy and the plan. This often has the added benefit of getting all of the questions out of the way at once. Many people will have the same questions and it can be inefficient to have everyone ask them of the manager one at a time.

Once the manager (or point person) has explained the policy to everyone, it should be brought up from time to time. How that is done is a decision every business will need to make.

However, I will tell you this from my own experience. If you mention something to people once, they'll remember it for a while and over time they will get out of habit and forget the training. That's just human nature.

To make it a reflex and to make it a routine and ingrained habit, someone needs to bring it up over and over and over and then keep bringing it up after that. Think about firefighters for a second. They don't learn a skill once and assume they're good forever. They drill. They practice. They repeat over and over. When the time comes, because of all this preparation, they're ready.

That is the job of your point person, whoever that is. Their job is to take this policy and turn it into a reliable company culture. They do that through communication, meetings, coaching and by always keeping carding front in center in the minds of every team member.


## Conclusion

Hopefully, now that we're at the end of this chapter, you know a bit more about ID types you might encounter and you have a rough outline of a carding policy and how to implement it.

This will be your plan. Don't worry if it's rough right now. There is time to refine it and you know where to get more information and guidance to help you do that.

The rest of this book will be dedicated to putting that plan into action with solid practices. In the chapters that follow, we are going to talk about how to card people properly, how to make that a reflex and how to catch people with fake IDs. We will tie it all up at the end with a discussion of what to do when you catch someone with a fake ID.

Let's get started!

## Chapter 2: Proper Carding Procedures

In this chapter we are actually going to talk about how to card people and what you should be looking for when you properly examine an ID. To start, I am going to assume that you know nothing about IDs or examining them. For those of my readers who do have experience with carding, please bear with me. This introductory approach is necessary for any inexperienced reader. There is a very real possibility that this book will be read by people who just bought a bar or a marijuana store and need this basic approach.

Even if you have years of experience examining IDs, I would recommend that you read through the following sections anyway. If you are reading this book, you may wind up **TEACHING** this material at some point in the future and a refresher may prove a useful investment.

## ID Checking Guide

The very first thing I want to talk about is an ID checking guide. There is a reason I have put this front and center in this chapter. That is, because I consider this to be the most important tool you can give your employees when checking IDs.

IDs and the world of carding are fluid and dynamic. They're always changing. New IDs are always coming out. New fakes are always coming out. You can't learn this stuff once and then rely on it forever. Carding and preventing underage drinking require ongoing, continuing training.

To achieve this simply and easily, you need to get an ID reference guide.

An ID reference guide is simply a book that is put out on an annual basis that gives information about all the IDs that are circulating in the United States. All fifty states and all five territories and districts will be in there as well. They often include Canadian and Mexican IDs as well.

There will be information on each state and each of the IDs they currently issue. It's very common for a state to issue several forms of ID as new models are phased in and old ones are phased out. There will be pictures and more importantly, model specific information like UV features, ghost pictures, ghost writing, tactile features and all the other information your front line servers, bartenders, bouncers, security and retail staff need to know.

You should have multiple copies of these books. They should live in a set place and should be readily accessible when they are needed. They're like a fire extinguisher. You don't want to have to go looking for them when they are needed.

I always have a number of these guides out on the floor and behind the bar. More importantly, I always have one more in my desk. I keep it locked away with other important backups. The truth is, things get lost in a restaurant environment. If I ever have to pull out that emergency copy, I know to order another one right away.

You can find these resources online. Just do a search for "ID checking guide" and you will have plenty of places willing to sell you one. If you can sign up for a plan where they just send you the next one when it comes out, I would recommend that too. It's one less thing you have to worry about.

## Generic ID Elements

Before we talk about ID features and how to examine them, as well as how to spot fake IDs, it would be best if we established a bit of a vocabulary. These phrases will be common throughout the rest of the book. They will also be useful when you're carding people and when you're teaching employees how to card properly

## Picture

Every ID that I have ever been presented in a professional capacity has a picture. IDs that do not have photos like insurance cards and credit cards should never be considered as proper ID. Passports, driver's licenses, military IDs, and tribal IDs all have photos on them.

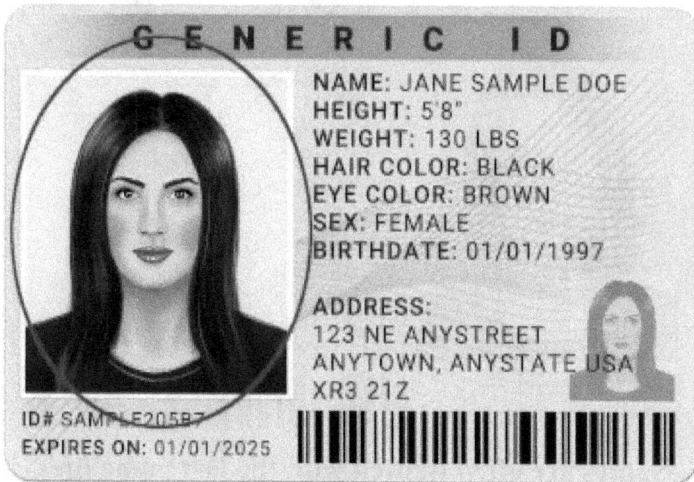

**The picture is the dominant feature on an ID.**

There can often be more going on in a photo than you would expect and I have spotted fake IDs from the photos alone. We will talk more about this in the future.

**Name**

Every ID you look at should have a name on it. In most cases it will be a family name, first name and middle name. Often, the name will be printed in more than one place to make altering an ID more difficult. Sometimes the person's name will be a part of the record number, again to make altering more difficult.

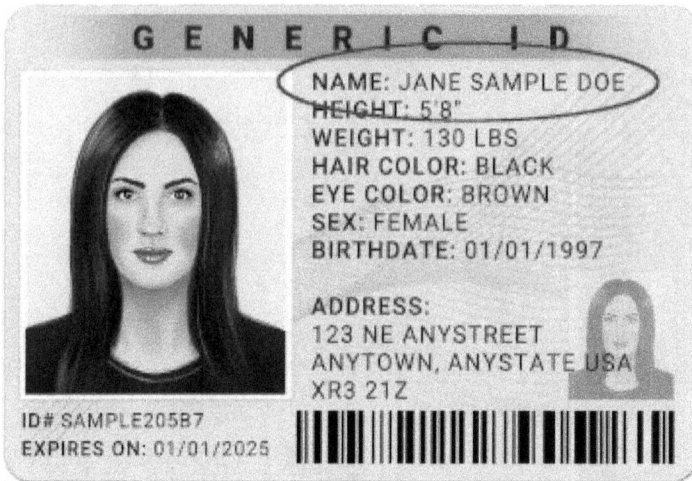

**Names are often written with the last name first.**

## Record Number

We live in a modern digital age with vast amounts of data stored on computers. To help with data storage, every ID that is issued, is issued a record number to go along with it. It is a combination of numbers and letters that is unique to that ID. At times, like when you are presented with a temporary paper ID as well as an expired driver's license, you will need to find and compare the record numbers.

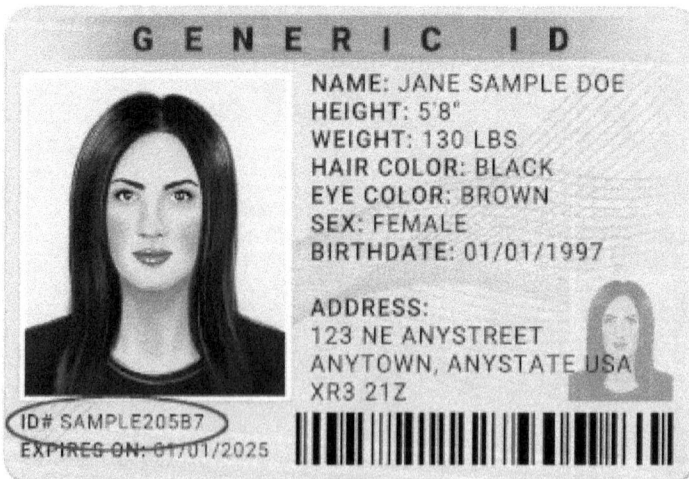

**Every ID has a unique record number.**

## Address

Some IDs will not have an address. Passports for example, do not have addresses. They do not link to an address the way a driver's license does. However, all of the driver's licenses and ID cards issued in the United States will have an address attached to them.

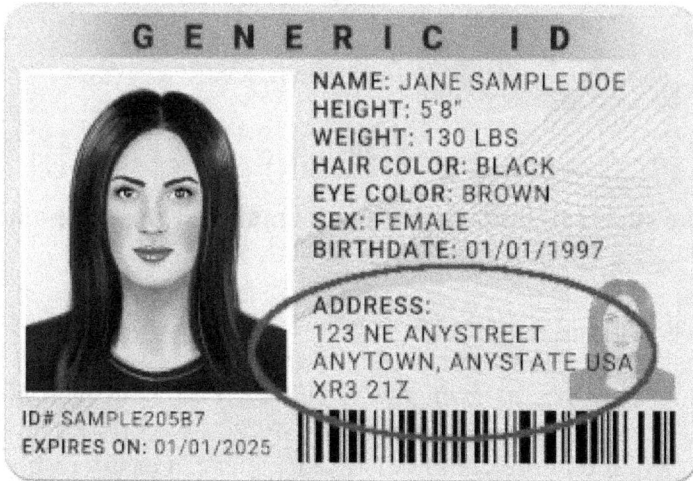

**Address information can be used to catch fake IDs.**

This can be a useful bit of information during the screening process. We will talk about ways to use this information to catch fakes later, but I can tell you, I have found fake IDs simply by reading the address.

## Birth date

For the purpose at hand, there is no more critical piece of information on an ID than the birth date. The whole reason you are reading this is because your business offers services that are not available to people who are below a certain age. You will look at, think about and make a decision concerning the birth date on every ID you examine.

Fortunately, many IDs make the birthdate prominent for this fact. Some are considerate enough to put the birthdate in a bright red box.

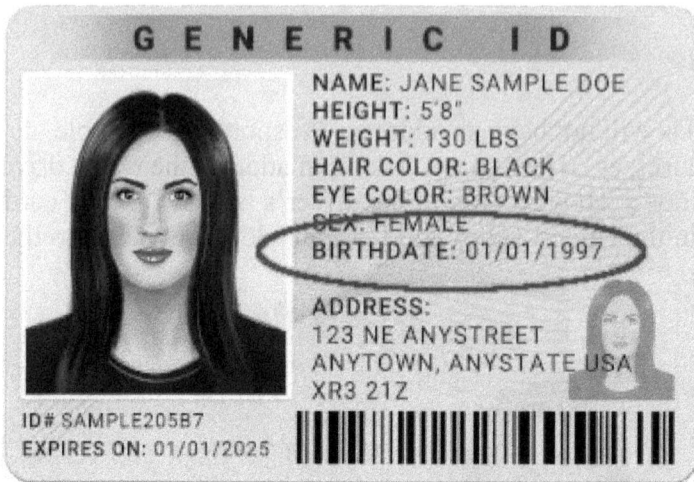

**GENERIC ID**

NAME: JANE SAMPLE DOE
HEIGHT: 5'8"
WEIGHT: 130 LBS
HAIR COLOR: BLACK
EYE COLOR: BROWN
SEX: FEMALE
BIRTHDATE: 01/01/1997

ADDRESS:
123 NE ANYSTREET
ANYTOWN, ANYSTATE USA
XR3 21Z

ID# SAMPLE205B7
EXPIRES ON: 01/01/2025

**Make sure you understand the format that the birthdate is written in to avoid costly mistakes.**

I feel that I should point out to you that there are also a variety of ways to display dates in the world. In the United States, most IDs that I have seen use the format MM-DD-YYYY. However, in Europe, Australia and Canada the format YYYY-MM-DD or DD-MM-YYYY are more commonly used. This can easily result in a misreading of the date if you are unfamiliar with this fact.

As this book is mostly intended for an American audience, I will be using MM-DD-YYYY for any dates listed from this point.

**Expiration date**

Most identification has a date when it expires. As of this writing, I do actually know of some ID types that do not expire. That may change in the future so I will not list them here as it may cause confusion in the years to come. However, the vast majority of IDs do expire at some point.

NAME: JANE SAMPLE DOE
HEIGHT: 5'8"
WEIGHT: 130 LBS
HAIR COLOR: BLACK
EYE COLOR: BROWN
SEX: FEMALE
BIRTHDATE: 01/01/1997

ADDRESS:
123 NE ANYSTREET
ANYTOWN, ANYSTATE USA
XR3 21Z

ID# SAMPLE2056F
EXPIRES ON: 01/01/2025

**The expiration date is an essential piece of information on an ID.**

After the expiration date, the ID is no longer considered valid. Along with the birthdate, the expiration date is one of the most important pieces of information that you will need to examine each and every time you card someone.

This information is often part of ID sting operations that are run by local law enforcement. They will send someone into a bar with an expired ID. They will present the ID as required. If they are served after presenting the expired ID, the employee and the business can be cited.

There is a bit of a technical point about the expiration date that I feel we should discuss.

In my career, in professional settings, I have found people arguing with me about whether an ID expires on the listed date or at the conclusion of that listed date. I will illustrate.

As an example, let's assume we have an ID that has a listed expiration date of 06-15-2021.

Now, does the ID expire at 12:01 AM on 06-15-2021? Or does it expire at the conclusion of 06-15-2021?

It's a good question that may be legally relevant.

The answer is there is no simple answer. There are just too many different IDs out there for any one person to know with 100% certainty. It's entirely possible that different states have different opinions on the matter.

The fact is, I can't give you a guarantee either way, but I will tell you how I have handled it through my career.

Unless an ID says "Valid through" on it, I assume that the ID expires at 12:01 AM on the date listed on it. Referring back to our example, the ID in question, in my opinion, would expire at 12:01 AM on the morning of 06-15-2021. At that point, it would no longer be valid and could not be used as proof of age.

## Issue date

The issue date is another piece of information that is on some types of identification. This is the day on which the issuing authority (like a Department of Motor Vehicles) sent it out to the person it identifies. In most cases, the issue date will be in the same format as the birth date and the expiration date.

I do not use the issue date as part of my process for verifying age. Where the issue date is especially useful is in spotting fake IDs. We will talk more about this in the next chapter.

## Physical description

Most forms of identification will have a physical description that goes along with the picture. The usual metrics will be height, weight, hair color and eye color.

It can be good to pay attention to this information if you suspect an ID is fake. Weight, hair color and even eye color are easily changed in the modern world. Height is another matter. Women may add a few inches with heels from time to time, but as a whole, height is generally constant.

**Physical characteristics are added to IDs to help you verify identity.**

If someone's ID says they are 6'5" and they are clearly 5'2", you should begin asking a lot of questions. We will discuss what to ask and how to interpret the responses in the next chapter as well.

**Cardstock**

IDs are printed documents. They are printed on something before they are given to the person that they identify. That "something" is known as the cardstock. Passports are printed on plastic laminated paper. Driver's licenses are printed on plastic.

There are many different types of cardstock that are used to issue driver's licenses. I would invite you, at this point, to go get your ID from your wallet. Flex it in your hands (don't break it) like in the following image:

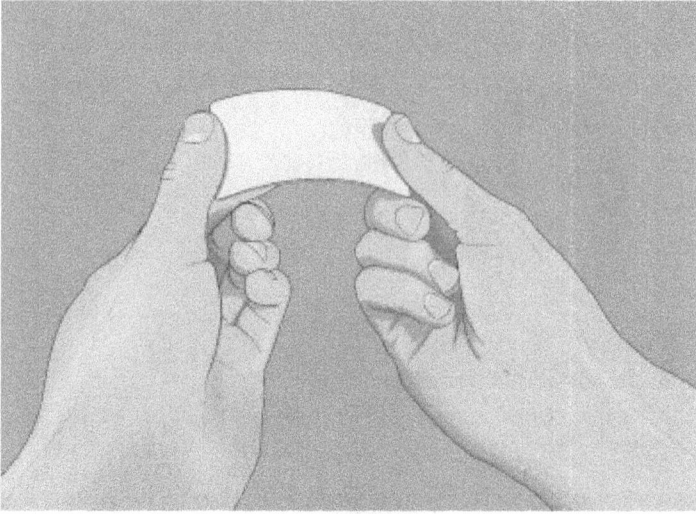

**Flexing every ID you are presented with will teach you how an ID should "feel".**

How does it feel?

As you go through your career, I would recommend that you make a habit of carefully flexing every ID that you get. It will help accustom you to what real ID cardstock feels like and it will make you better at spotting fake IDs.

**Magnetic strip, Barcode & RFID tags**

Modern IDs do not just have information printed on them. They also have information encoded on them. This is done in three different ways. They are magnetic strips, barcodes and using RFID chips. This information can be relevant to you if your business is equipped with scanning equipment as part of your carding policy and procedures.

Magnetic strips use the same technology that was used on VHS tapes and mixtapes. Information is encoded in bits of magnet strip that is printed on an ID. If you take out a credit card and look at the back of you, that black strip about a half inch wide is the magnetic strip.

**Magnetic strips are an inexpensive technology to encode information on an ID.**

Magnetic strips have been popular in years past because the technology is older and more accessible. However, using the right technology it is possible to change this information or to erase it. This is the same idea as "taping over" a cassette tape.

When I say "barcode" I am using it as a catch all term. What I really mean is non-magnetic patterns that are read optically with a laser or other scanner. This can be a barcode like what you would find on a can of beans in the grocery store. It can also be more complicated patterns that are similar to a QR code.

**Barcodes are a way of digitally encoding information on an ID.**

Barcodes are taking over the encoded information on most IDs that I am familiar with. The price of optical scanners has been falling for years and the technology is becoming cheaper. Also, it is much harder to alter the printed information in a barcode. The information may look chaotic, but those lines and dots are all carefully placed with mathematical precision.

The last method for encoding information on an ID is with an RFID chip. This is the youngest and most expensive technology of the three I have listed. Although, prices are falling and the amount of precision that this technology offers will, in my opinion, make it the ID tech of the future.

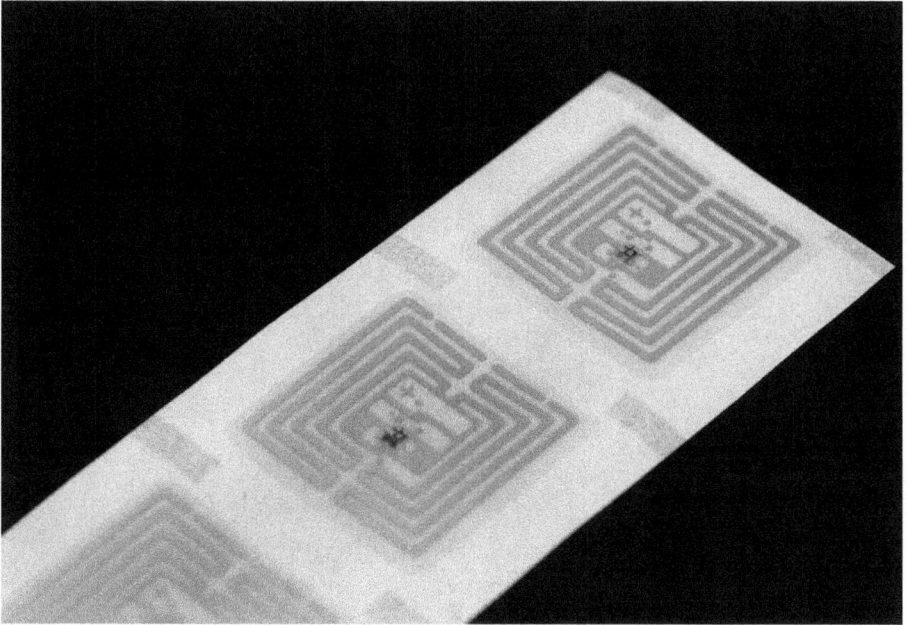

**RFID tags like these ones can be used to store information in IDs like passports.**

RFID stands for "Radio Frequency Identification". These are very small electronic circuits that store information and "broadcast" it when they interact with a special electromagnetic (EM) field.

What the heck does that mean?

It means, a scanner sends out a radio signal like a TV remote, the chip reacts to it and sends one back with information attached encoded in it. The scanner receives the information and displays it, nicely formatted, on a screen.

I have not personally heard of this technology being used on driver's licenses or identity cards, as of this writing. I'm quite certain that that will begin happening very soon. Where I have seen it is on passports. Modern passports have these chips and will react to an EM signal with the info.

**The small symbol under "The United States of America" indicated that this passport carries an RFID tag with digital information encoded on it.**

There is equipment out there that is fairly priced that will allow you to scan this information.

Do you need it?

The answer to that depends a lot on your business. If your business sees a large amount of passports like an international resort or an airport bar, this may be appropriate. In my experience, I have only ever encountered one fake passport (we will talk about this in Chapter 3) and it was incredibly obvious. There was no need to scan it. I knew immediately that it was fake.

From everything I have ever encountered in my career, passports are incredibly hard to forge and most of your underage drinkers will have neither the inclination nor the resources to obtain one. However, as with all the aspects of your carding policy and procedures, I will leave the final decision to you.

## UV Features

Modern IDs are often printed with UV features that help make them harder to counterfeit.  UV features are parts of the ID that respond to ultraviolet (UV) light.  THe features vary quite a bit.  They can be wavy lines, state seals, decorative images like birds, faces (Abraham Lincoln, for example) ghost images (State of California as of this printing).

**UV Features, like on this money offer another way to check IDs and to often spot fake ones.**

Checking the UV features is an incredibly important part of proper carding.  I have caught many fake IDs, personally, just by examining and knowing what the proper UV features are.  Forgers often make mistakes or assign less importance to this part of a fake ID.

To check the UV features of an ID, you will need a UV light.  These are easy to come buy and you can buy them online for only a few dollars.  Personally, I consider these to be part of a standard kit of ID checking tools.  If you have one, carry it and use it.  If you do not, get one and then carry and use it.

**A reliable UV flashlight like this one should be standard
equipment for anyone who checks IDs.**

Honestly, just the act of shining a UV light on IDs as you check
them will give the impression of heightened scrutiny and will
discourage some people with fakes. This is definitely an area where
an ounce of prevention is worth a pound of cure.

**Ghost Image**

Ghost images have become incredibly common on American IDs in
the last ten years and they can help you spot fakes and other
irregularities.

A ghost image is a small, largely transparent version of the main
portrait on an ID. They're the same image as the main one, just
smaller and semi-transparent. This more transparent aspect gives
rise to the term "ghost image".

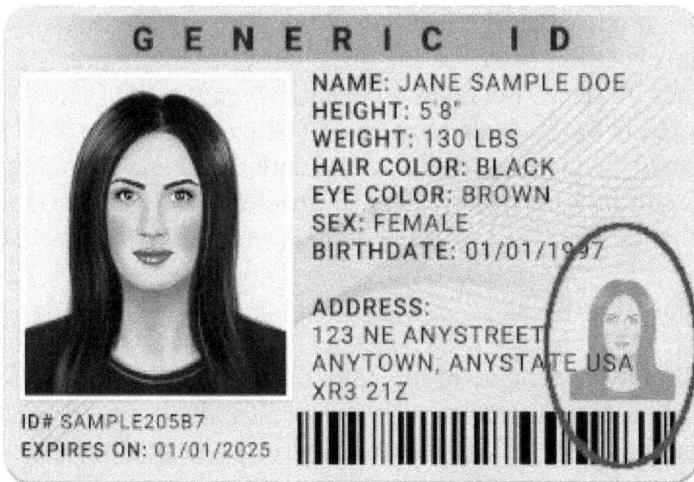

GENERIC ID

NAME: JANE SAMPLE DOE
HEIGHT: 5'8"
WEIGHT: 130 LBS
HAIR COLOR: BLACK
EYE COLOR: BROWN
SEX: FEMALE
BIRTHDATE: 01/01/1997

ADDRESS:
123 NE ANYSTREET
ANYTOWN, ANYSTATE USA
XR3 21Z

ID# SAMPLE205B7
EXPIRES ON: 01/01/2025

**Ghost images are small, transparent images that are added to many IDs.**

When you are examining an ID, always compare all of the portraits. There is always the main one, there is often a ghost image and sometimes there is a smaller, "mini portrait" as well. Look at each one. Do they match? I have seen bad fakes where they do not. Some forger was phoning it in and wasn't paying attention and left the old picture intact.

That one was easy to spot, but only because I take a detail oriented approach to carding every time. I advise you to adopt the same approach. Take your time, study the details and make the right decision. Don't let anyone rush, bully or intimidate you. Remember, your license and your livelihood are on the line. That makes it your show!

**Ghost Features**

In addition to ghost images, there can also be ghost features on and ID. These are semi-transparent security features like holograms and other decorative features that only become visible when looked at a certain way. Again, these are hard to duplicate by design and as such are often incorrect with fake IDs.

I can't give you every detail on every ID's ghost features. Each IDs features will be listed in the ID checking guide you buy. I recommend you learn the features of the IDs you see most commonly. Often these are the ones that you will be presented and sometimes these are the fakes. The most common ID I have confiscated is from a state immediately adjacent to mine. It's not from across the country. It's a commonplace ID and I would guess is above scrutiny for many of my ID checking colleagues. Don't be one of them.

## Redundant Pictures

Many IDs have a redundant image in addition to or instead of a ghost image. A redundant image is just a smaller, second version of the main photo on the ID. If someone tries to print a new photo image on an ID, with a redundant image, they have to alter two. This is much harder.

## Holograms

A hologram is a three dimensional illusion that is created with special inks and printing patterns. On IDs they can be simple lines that look like they're popping out of the ID or they can be complicated features like state seals.

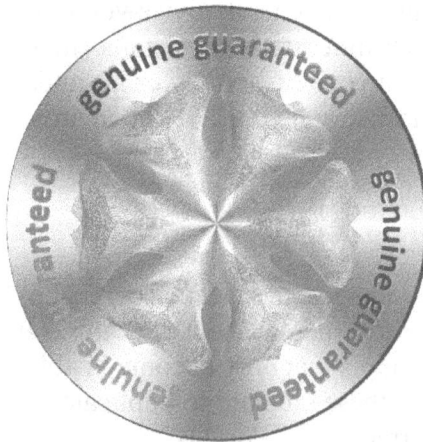

**Holograms like this one are used on many types of IDs as an enhanced security feature.**

An ID might have no holograms and instead only have UV features. Some have both and they're worth paying attention to. In my career I have seen many IDs that should have holograms and did not. That's when I knew they were fake.

It takes only a fraction of a second to examine a hologram, but it is a very effective test at catching some fake IDs.

**Tactile Features**

Some IDs are perfectly flat and when you run your finger over them (more on this later when we talk about fakes IDs) you will and should feel nothing. Some however, have features that you're supposed to feel. This is just another layer of complexity that is designed to thwart forgers.

These are called "tactile features".

One example, as of this writing, is the state of California. On current (2020) California IDs, the signature is actually a laser etched feature that creates a rough surface for your finger to catch on. If you run your finger over a California and feel nothing, you have a suspect ID in your hands.

Again, there are many IDs with new ones coming out every year. There are new security features on all of these. Take a minute and think about the IDs you see often. Then, go get your ID guide and see what tactile features are present. Remember them. Check for them.

**Proper Carding Procedures - Step By Step**

Now that you have a general knowledge of the elements on an ID that you will need to look at, pay attention to and examine, let's talk about how you actually go about carding someone. It's more complicated than it would seem at first blush. Also, I would encourage you to think of this as a skill just like any other. You have to practice to get better and as you keep practicing, your skills will improve.

One last bit I'd like to emphasise before you really get to the heart of the matter is to remind anyone and everyone, to ask questions. If something looks off, if something is strange, unfamiliar or seems out of place, ask someone with more experience. Just have them give it a second look. With this stuff, it's always, always, always better to be safe than sorry. The liability and legal and financial consequences of failure are just not worth it!

Moving on…

OK. So imagine that someone walks into your business and you decide that they're a person you need to card. What do you do?

There's a simple process you should follow. Before we get into that though, I want to discuss how you should use this procedure.

You should make it a habit to follow this procedure each and every time you ask for someone's ID. Memorize the steps now, follow them as you work, and they will soon become second nature.

## Step 1: Ask them for their ID

Depending on your work situation, you may card someone at several different points. If you work in a bar or marijuana shop, you will ask the customer for ID immediately when they attempt to enter an age restricted area.

If you work in a convenience store or grocery store that sells beer and wine, you may not ask for ID until they are at the point of sale.

Either way, the process is the same.

Politely ask them if they have ID.

It seems like a simple concept, but it's not always the case. I have personally seen many employees in the hospitality and service industry ask for ID by yelling across a bar at customers. I have been in convenience and grocery stores where cashiers have made no secret of their unfriendliness when asking for ID.

Long story short, I can point to lots of examples of rudeness at this point in the carding process.

All I will say is that at this point, you don't know who the person you are asking for ID is. That's why you're asking for an ID. There is a very good chance that after they provide their ID, they will be allowed to proceed and at that point, will be a paying customer in your business or your place of employment.

My advice is to always begin that relationship on a positive note and to conduct yourself professionally right from start.

Usually, I say something like:

"Sorry guys, but do you have your IDs?"

Or

"Excuse me guys, but can I check your ID?"

The apology and a little courtesy are usually accepted and the ID checking is looked at as a formality. We will talk about when the guests are not friendly, flatly rude or even confrontational in the next section.

## Step 2: Have them remove their ID from their wallet

A lot of the time when you ask for someone's ID, they'll flash their wallet at you like they're a cop on an old TV show.

For our purposes, that isn't going to work. When trying to examine an ID without removing it from a wallet, you cannot examine many of the features.

For example, in my personal experience looking at IDs in a wallet, the expiration date is often covered. This is an essential date to check. If you can't check it because it's covered, you're not doing your job.

Pay attention when they take the ID out. I have also personally seen people pull out their fake ID with their real ID underneath.

If you see another ID underneath, ask to see it too. Nine times out of ten, it will be their old expired ID. A lot of people seem to carry these. If it's not that, it could be an issue.

Ask to see both IDs. If everything is legitimate, and it's an old expired ID, they'll have no trouble letting you look at it.

If, on the other hand they get nervous, refuse, start making excuses or start giving you attitude, this could be signs that something is wrong.

In situations like that, most of the time I would refuse service. If you're not empowered to refuse service, ask for help. Get your manager involved and have them help you to make educated, wise decisions. Having another person there will help to keep any odd situation calm as well.

## Step 3 - Physical Examination

Once you have the ID out of their wallet, you can hold it, touch it and inspect it physically. This involves two simple procedures that are quick but can tell you many things about the ID.

The first thing you should do is flex the ID itself, like in the following picture:

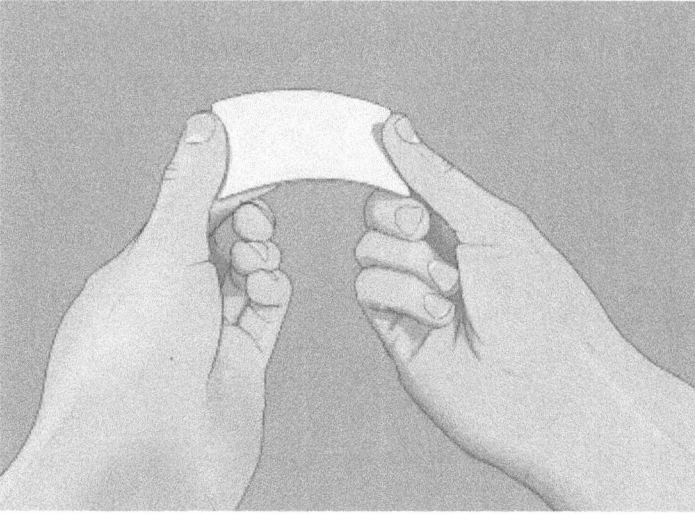

**Flex every ID you get.  Fake IDs often have a different "feel" than real IDs.**

Legitimate, real IDs are printed on specially made, specific plastic cardstock.  While this material can vary from state to state, you will quickly get used to the feel of the material.  You will know how thick it should be and how it should react to you flexing it.
Each ID you flex, helps to train your brain to remember how it "should" feel.  I promise you, when you run into a fake ID that is printed on cheap, thin cardstock, you will know the difference.  I first became suspicious of many of the fake IDs I caught because the flex of the cardstock was wrong.  It didn't feel like it "should" have.

The second step in a physical examination is to run your thumb over the face of the ID.  The following picture shows how to do this.

**Running your thumb over the face of an ID will quickly identify tactile features or signs of alteration.**

Run your thumb back and forth over the face of the ID. You're doing this for two reasons and you're looking for two things. Do you remember those tactile features from the last chapter? This is how you look for them. Features like raised, laser engraved signatures will be very obvious to your thumb. If they're not there and they should be, your suspicions should immediately go up.

You're also looking for tactile features that shouldn't be there. Examples of these would be raised bubbles or air pockets on the ID. You can also feel cuts in the laminate or if another laminate layer has been added to the ID. These layers are less than a millimeter thick and can be easily missed by your eye in a dark bar or restaurant, but your finger will feel them instantly.

**Punches, Holes, Clips & Cancellations?**

After you run your thumb over the ID, you need to look for punches, holes, or clips that indicate that an ID is no longer valid. If an ID is invalid, you cannot (and should not) accept it as proof of age.

What is a hole, punch or clip?

A hole is a hole like you would find on a piece of notebook paper for school. They're made with the same tool. The presence of a hole like this is a way for government authorities (think DMVs, police, courts) to cancel the ID. I have seen these holes many times.

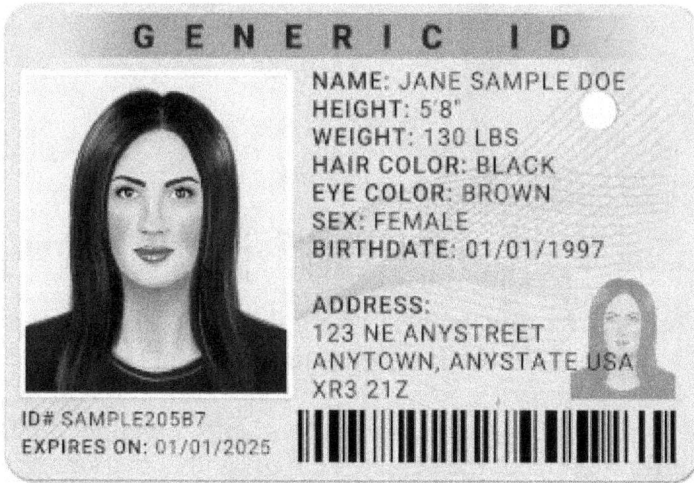

**An example of a holed ID. Notice the white, circular hole in the top right corner of the ID.**

A punch is a little bit different. Punched IDs usually are a smaller diamond sized hole that has been made in the ID. I have seen these many times and they are usually smaller and are harder to see so look carefully and feel for them with your thumb. These likewise cancel the ID and make them invalid.

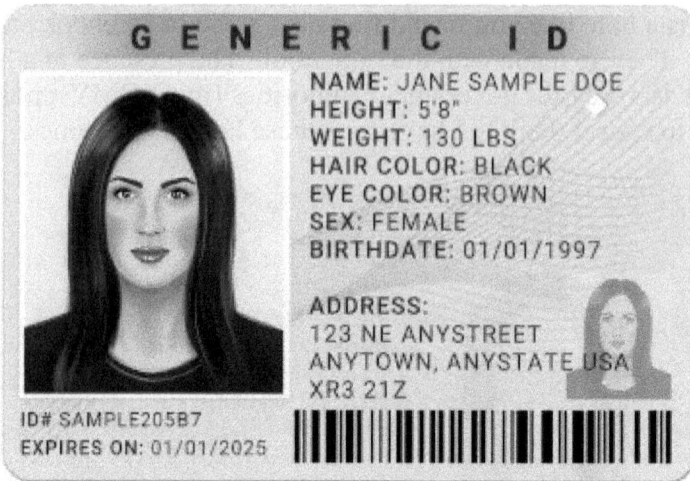

**An example of a punched ID.  Note the small diamond shaped hole in the top right corner of the ID.**

The last modification you are likely to run into is a clipped ID. When an ID is clipped, the corner is cut off with a pair of scissors. These are pretty easy to see and you will run into this.

**An example of a clipped ID.**

Why does this happen?

This happens for two reasons generally.  The first is someone is renewing their ID before the expiration date.  SInce IDs are usually mailed out these days, this ID can be used as a way to identify themselves until the new ID arrives.

The other is more serious. The other reasons that this happens usually has to do with drunk driving or other license suspension related issues. The ID is holed or punched to signify this while a matter is unresolved before the courts.

It is unlikely you will know which one applies when you are checking ID. That's not your business anyway.

Either way, it will mean that you need to decline the ID since it is invalid. Additionally, there can be minor related issues with this. I have known more than one sister who gave her old, expired, punched ID to her younger, similar looking sister to use when she was underage.

Refusing service will eliminate these issues as well as the legal uncertainty. Remember, if things are unclear, your safest bet is always to politely and professionally decline the ID.

## Step 4 - Visual Inspection

With a visual inspection, you examine the ID with your eyes and you use your eyes to process the information on the ID and make sure it matches the person standing in front of you.

## Flashlights

We will get into how to methodically do this, but first I want to talk about setting yourself up to be successful. When we talked about the physical inspection I talked about how your thumb could feel things you eyes would miss in a dark bar or restaurant. Well, now you do need your eyes and you still may be in that dark bar or restaurant.

How do you solve this problem?

You get a tool. Specifically a flashlight.

**UV flashlights are an essential tool for effective ID checking.
Many can switch between UV and visible light too.**

I would recommend that every employee who is responsible for checking IDs be expected to carry a flashlight. I do not mean their phone. They have flashlights, but pulling them out in a service context is inappropriate, creates management issues and just takes too long. Instead, I would require them to carry small, powerful, discrete LED flashlights that have one button activation. Many models will switch between UV and visual light and they are worth their weight in gold when it comes to ID checking.

Some bar owners will be tempted to provide a team flashlight for everyone to use. I have a dim view of this idea. In my experience, when everyone is responsible for a flashlight, no one is responsible for it. They have a tendency to wander off, lose their batteries, to have dead batteries or to be behind the bar where they are of no practical use to anyone.

I recommend that each person who is responsible for carding be required to have a flashlight as part of their uniform. It's a necessary tool and it's not unreasonable to require them to provide one. Also, if they have to spend money on one, employees will generally take better care of them. Also, at the end of the day, you can often get 2 for $10 so the burden is minimal.

As a manager, I always had one or two extra flashlights locked up in my office. If servers forgot theirs, I would sell them one at cost. That way they'd have two and it helped them to remember to bring one on their next shift.

## Conducting Visual Inspection

## 1. The Picture

To start the visual inspection, shine your light on the ID. Take a second and look at it. Look for any abnormalities on the face of the ID. Ask yourself:

- Does everything look like it should?
- Are the colors the right shade?
- Are they as bright as they should be?
- Do you see any bubbles, cuts or other marks that indicate the ID has been altered?
- Do all the fonts match?

What's that about fonts? Fonts on an ID are standardized. They should be consistent across the ID. If they aren't for some reason you should be suspicious.

Now look at the picture. This is the most important part of the visual inspection. The picture contains more information than the rest of the ID combined.

Look at the picture. Try to soak it in and examine it. Study the features of the person shown. Pay close attention to their eyes, ther nose and how they sit on the face.

Then hold the ID so you can see the person and the picture at the same time.
This will allow you to compare and cross reference the photo with the person's actual face

This can be challenging. Some people will have gotten an ID card when they were 15 and they are using it (legally) when they are 22.

People cut, die and shave their hair. People grow beards. It may be the same person, but it can take your brain a second to decide this.

Take your time, don't rush this part. Study the eyes and nose and how they sit on the face. Soak the picture and the person in front of you in.

Close should not count. I have known plenty of big sisters who passed their old ID to their little sister. Sisters and brothers look alike. Don't fall for this. I have also seen plenty of brash college kids hand their old ID to their friend to try and pass off. Don't fall for that either. Stop. Study. Examine. Compare. And Don't Rush!

Now is also when you should study any redundant image. Does it match the big image on the ID and does it match the person in front of you?

If for some reason you decide that the person in front of you isn't the one on the ID, I would refuse service.

**Physical Characteristics**

Beyond just the picture, there are other pieces of information on many IDs that can be used to verify the person in front of you. IDs that you will encounter often include, height, weight, eye color and hair color.

Weight, eye color and hair color can all fluctuate and change easily. Height is another matter.

Although people can and do wear shoes that change their height, height is pretty hard to change. This makes any height data listed on the ID very useful to us. Compare the height on the ID to the person standing in front of you. Ask yourself:

- Do they match?
- If there is some fluctuation is it the kind of thing that a pair of high heels might explain?
- Are they wearing high heels?

If something doesn't add up, you should become more suspicious. We will talk more about how to challenge people when something doesn't add up or is unclear in the next chapter.

**Step 5 - Verify The Dates**

After confirming that the person standing in front of you is the person shown in the ID, there are two dates that need to be verified to complete the carding process. These dates are the birthdate and the expiration date.

There are specific considerations that go into verifying each date.

**Birthdate**

When carding someone, start with the birthdate. This will tell you if the person is old enough and whether or not you should proceed to the expiration date.

Generally, you will see this date written in numerical format that looks like one of the following:

- MM/DD/YYYY - Month first, then day, then year in four digit form

- MM/DD/YY - Month first, then day, then year in two digit format

- DD/MM/YYYY - Day first, then month, then year in four digit format

- DD/MM/YY - Day first, then month, then year in two digit format

As you can see, there is more than one way to write a birthdate and this can cause confusion if you are unaware of which format is being used.

In the United States, it is more common to see the month first format. However, in the rest of the world, it is more common to use the day first, month second format. This can cause a risk of error in cases where the ID is written in a language that you cannot read. This is a prime reason you should not accept IDs you can't read.

If you see a date that reads "06/05/1999" and the ID is written in a language you cannot read, does that mean June 5th, 1997 or May, 6th 1997? That variation can mean the difference between someone being old enough and someone being too young to legally drink or buy marijuana. It can also make a sale legal or illegal.

It can also mean the difference between you committing a punishable criminal act or just doing your job.

As a rule, if you cannot tell which date format is being used and there is some doubt as to whether someone is old enough, I would recommend declining service.

**Expiration Date**

The birth date, properly read and understood, will tell you whether someone is old enough to participate in a legally controlled transaction or service. The expiration date will tell you whether you can legally accept an ID at all.

Jurisdictions require an ID to be legally valid and unexpired for you to accept it. You should know what your regulating authority requires for your locality. Send them an email so you get your answer in writing. This is good due diligence that creates a documented record that may be useful at some point in the future.

The expiration date will usually be written in the same format as the birth date. All of the same format considerations that are at play with the birthdate will apply to the expiration date as well. If you don't know or are unsure of the format, and that could impact whether the ID is valid or not, I would encourage you to error on the side of caution and decline accepting the ID.

With expiration dates, there is another concern. This has to do with wording.

I have run into two phrases with expiration dates. They differ and it makes a big difference which one is being used. The two phrases that I have seen used are:

- "Expires on"

and

- "Valid through"

Sometimes formatting will only allow something short like:

- "Expires"

or

- "EXP"

What exactly do these mean?

When teaching this concept, I like to use milk as an example.

Imagine you have milk in your refrigerator and there is a date on it. Let's imagine it says:

- "January 15th, 2015"

Let's imagine it's written nice and clearly like this, when in reality, this will not be true with an ID.

Now, imagine it is 12:00 PM on January 15, 2015. Is the milk good?

It depends on what is written above that date. If it says "Expires on", I would assume that the milk expired at 12:01 AM that morning and it has been expired for almost 12 hours.

Now, on the other hand, if it says "Valid through: January 15th, 2015", it's an entirely different matter. Valid through means that the milk is valid all day January 15th, 2015 and only expires at 12:01 AM on the morning of January 16th, 2015.

Two little words mean a whole day's difference in when the milk expires.

Two little words mean a whole day's difference in when and ID expires too.

I don't bring this up idly. If you check IDs long enough, you will run into an unclear situation and somebody who will argue these semantics with you. It's happened to me many times when I'm busy and do not have time to discuss it in detail.

I always operate as though an ID expires at 12:01 AM of the date that is printed on it, unless there is VERY CLEAR wording that makes me confident it is valid through that date.

If you show up in my restaurant at 12:00 PM on January 15, 2015 with an ID that says "Expires On: 01/15/2015" I will assume the ID expired at 12:01 AM that morning. I will decline service at that point because the ID is expired.
That is also what I will do if it is unclear and says something like "EXP" or "Expires".

People will argue with you that you're wrong. It's happened to me many times. No one likes being turned away or denied service. Frankly, you might be. However, you're protecting you, your employer and your job.

If you find yourself in this situation, stay calm. Remain polite and professional. If you're not the manager, bring the manager into the situation as backup to resolve the problem.

Remember, if you assume wrong with carding, it can cost you a lot! It's always best to error on the side of caution.

For managers, to help employees to be successful, I would recommend getting a "born on date" clock.

These clocks, if used properly will display the date someone has to have been born to be old enough to do something. Employees can easily reference it when checking an ID. It acts as a double check and will help reduce costly errors and ID mistakes when people lose track of the date.

Put it on the wall in an area where the employees who will be doing carding can see it. If this happens in more than one place, get more than one clock.

**Step 6 - Check the printed security features.**

Now it's time to check those printed security features like holograms, ghost images and UV features. Take just a second or two to look for them and examine them. Make this part of your process. If you have taken my advice and have a UV flashlight, shine it on the ID.

If you're familiar with an ID, you will most likely know what the features should be and whether they are correct. If you are not familiar with an ID, you can look it up in your reference books.

This may take an extra minute, but this is a good investment in your professional development. Over time, you will become better at finding these features, you will be able to tell more quickly when something is not as it should be and you will be able to spot fake IDs much quicker.

Many of the times I have spotted fake IDs, it has been because of inconsistencies and errors in the printed security features. Things lit up that shouldn't have, there were UV ink drops messily spilled on the ID or seals that should light up didn't.

These features are worth paying attention to.

**Step 7 - Scan the ID (if applicable)**

When you scan an ID, you use a computer to access information stored on an ID in either a barcode or a magnetic strip. These computers can also be used to verify the dates on the IDs and act as a backup check to your own process.

When I entered the hospitality industry decades ago, scanners were very uncommon, large machines and were amazingly expensive. Only large chains like grocery stores had the resources to buy, implement and train their staff to use scanners.

Now, scanners are small, easy to use and relatively inexpensive. Reliable scanners can be purchased for less than $1000. They are easy to use and can prevent employees from making a simple mistake with a date that can easily cost $10,000.

If your place of employment has a scanner, use it every time, but don't get in the habit of relying on it or letting it do the majority of the work. It can help you avoid misreading a date or accepting an expired ID. They cannot check pictures and make sure that the person in front of you is the person on the ID, not their younger brother. That's still a human job that needs to be done - by you.

If you're a business owner or a manager, deciding to invest in a scanning system is a lot like making the decision about who to card. As a general rule, I am aware of no legal requirements that you buy and use a scanning system. Sometimes businesses can be required to use them if they have failed carding stings or have been cited for failing to properly card customers. Check with your licensing agency for the most current info.

That being said, if you're a business owner, especially one involved in high volume or retail sales of regulated products like marijuana, I would strongly encourage you to at least take a look at scanners and how they might fit into your business as an additional compliance tool. As costs continue to go down, their convenience and usefulness as an investment goes up.

**Secondary IDs**

At some point a customer will provide you with an ID that you just don't feel good about. Maybe they got the ID when they were 15 and they haven't updated it in 10 years. Maybe they dyed their hair purple, got a face tattoo and grew an enormous beard since then. When dealing with a business that is open to the public, you will see situations just like this.

So you're standing there holding an ID that you think COULD be the person in front of you but you're just not 100%. What do you do?

You ask for a secondary ID.

A secondary ID (often called backup ID) is an ID that is not acceptable on it's own either by law or house policy, but can be used as further evidence that someone is who they claim to be. Some examples of secondary ID would be:

- ATM, debit or credit cards
- Insurance documents like healthcare or auto insurance cards
- County issued documents like a concealed carry permit
- Social security cards

These documents are issued by trusted sources like banks, insurance companies and lesser governments like counties or even cities. They usually know and trust who their customer is and as a result, you can usually consider these, in addition to a primary ID you aren't 100% on, when deciding if someone has sufficiently proved their identity to you.

How do you ask for a secondary ID?

Personally, when I am unconvinced of someone's primary ID and I want a little more convincing, I will say something like:

"Do you have another form or ID too? Something like a bank card or insurance ID?"

If you word it like that you are doing yourself a favor. First, you're saying you need **_ANOTHER ID_**. Most of your customers will have no idea why you're asking for this. They may have never been in an age restricted business and may not understand. Then, you're suggesting to them some of the documents that you're hoping they can provide you in a problem solving way.

Most people will have some form of secondary ID when you ask for it and will pull out several for you to choose from. When they do, take the secondary IDs and match up available information like the name, birthday, address or physical description. Do they all match? If they do, that is a strong case and a lot of evidence that the person in front of you is who they say they are.

However, when they say they don't have a secondary ID, which will likely happen at some point, it can be a big red flag.

I have seen plenty of people who hand me an ID and then when asked about secondary ID, they say they have nothing else with their name on it. That's odd in this day and age and is exactly what a kid with a fake ID with a fake name would say. Sometimes they would have a wallet that was an inch thick with cards and they would **STILL** say they had nothing else with their name on it. That's always a HUGE red flag.

As with everything you learn from this book, you will decide how to apply the knowledge and you will make your own decisions where you work. In my career, if anyone was ever unable to produce secondary ID, I would decline entry. It was as simple as that. It just isn't worth taking the chance.

**Expired IDs**

What do you do if someone presents you with an expired ID?

I won't speak to the law or legal matters in your particular area. For that, you should contact your regulating authority. In many cases, the law will require you to refuse to accept expired IDs. However, that may not be the case for every jurisdiction in the United States.

As a general rule, in my opinion, it's wise to refuse to accept expired IDs as a matter of house policy. This eliminates some potential problems in one quick policy decision.

Imagine for example that an older sister finds her old expired ID. She then gives it to her minor sister. Her younger sister who looks a lot like her then uses the expired ID to gain entry to your bar with her older sister. You have two IDs in this case, but only one person who is legally allowed to be in the bar. You have a liability and a compliance issue you could have easily avoided.

Even if it is legally permitted, I would recommend refusing to accept expired IDs.

**Temporary Paper IDs**

Many states in the United States have begun to issue temporary, paper IDs. This happens when someone either renews their ID online or through the mail or even in person at a licensing office. At the time of the renewal, the temporary, paper ID is issued while the official ID is produced and mailed to the owner.

If someone renews their ID in person at a licensing office, their old ID is usually punched. However, if they renew online or through the mail, this may not be the case. If a person's ID is not punched it may expire before they receive their new ID.

In either case the temporary, paper ID is generally to be used with the old expired or punched ID to establish identity. State laws will vary, but in my experience, the paper ID is generally not sufficient to establish identity and age on its own. If state law does permit it, I would recommend thinking seriously about setting a house policy that requires a temporary ID to be used with the old punched or expired ID.

Modern printers can be very powerful and it wouldn't be too hard to craft a fake temporary paper ID that could fool an unobservant bartender or bouncer.

Another problem with accepting temporary, paper IDs on their own is that many of them lack the security and even identity features, like pictures, that you will find on regular IDs. This makes accepting them a risky proposition.

Lastly, just like regular state issued IDs, each state has a different one and they're constantly changing. However, unlike regular IDs, there is no reference guide that helps you verify and identify these temporary IDs or their, if any, security features.

I once had a very confident young man try and convince me that Bolivia issued handwritten passports. He had modified one into a crude fake ID. If I didn't know better, I might have been tempted to believe him. Young people trying to sneak into bars can be clever and resourceful. I would not put it past the combined intelligence in a dorm building to craft a fake temporary ID in a scheme to get an underage friend into a bar for Taco Tuesday.

Avoid that by requiring the punched or expired ID as well as the temporary. It won't remove the need for vigilance. It will, however, make it harder for underage people to buy controlled substances or engage in regulated activities in your business.

**Minor Sting Operations Explained**

Before we move on to techniques for spotting fake IDs, let's take a look at minor sting operations, why they're important and how you can avoid the problems associated with them.

First, what is a minor sting operation?

A minor sting operation is when an underage person, working in partnership with law enforcement enters a licensed and regulated business with an invalid ID. If you run a convenience store, they may try to buy cigarettes. If you run a bar, they may try to order a drink. If you run a marijuana store, they may try to gain entry.

It is up to you, your employees, your policies and your training to catch this person before they are allowed to engage in a regulated activity. You need to spot the invalid ID and to refuse them access. Granting them access with the invalid ID is a failure of the minor sting and will result in fines and legal consequences.

Why does law enforcement conduct minor sting operations?

Law enforcement conducts minor sting operations as a way to ensure compliance by licensed businesses and their employees.

It makes sense. If people are aware that these operations happen and are fearful of failing one, it encourages diligent and effective carding. This applies equally to businesses, managers and employees.

I have encountered plenty of employees and even business owners who view these operations as an annoyance. I would encourage you to view them as a tool to help encourage legal compliance and attention to detail from your employees.

How is it decided where to conduct a minor sting operation?

There are two answers to this question and chances are both are in effect in your community.

The first answer is that any licensed establishment may be targeted as part of an ongoing and routine compliance check. Law enforcement may move around your community the way police in speed traps do. They'll show the flag in one part of town until they have made their presence felt and then will move to another area they haven't visited in a while. Then they will repeat the whole process all over again.

The other answer to that question is that businesses that are reported to be in violation of the law may be directly targeted as part of an investigation. For example, imagine that you own a convenience store and your clerk is selling beer to underage people and is not carding. If some of those underage people are caught drinking in a public park, usually law enforcement will ask where they got the beer. If the underage people say they bought it at your store, chances are good the police will report it to your licensing authority. They will then investigate. They may make a phone call and talk to you or they may just choose to launch a minor sting to test your compliance.

What kind of ID is used in a minor sting?

While I cannot tell you how every regulating authority in America conducts minor stings, I will speak to my personal experience. First, as a general rule minor stings do not use fake IDs or something else cooked up in a secret agent lab. The goal of these operations is usually diligent compliance and as such, they use real IDs that are invalid for the service or product you offer..

How are minor sting IDs invalid?

From my experience they are invalid in one of two ways. My understanding is the ID will be authentic, state issued ID in either case.

The ID will either be expired or the ID will show somebody's real birthday, but they will also be younger than someone who is legally allowed to buy a controlled substance or participate in a regulated activity.

This may not be an exhaustive list. It is certainly plausible that a regulating authority somewhere in America also uses somebody else's ID. This would be a realistic test of a clerk or bartender. Underage people who have a friend a year older than them do this all the time.

If you have more questions about this process or how it is conducted in your area, you should call your regulating authority. In fact, I would recommend you do that even if you think you know how it works. Get the facts that are specific to your location now, before you need them.  Ask a lot of questions and make sure you understand.

See if you can get them to send you some printed material that you can distribute to your staff.  It would make excellent ongoing training  and reference material for your compliance program and carding policy.  If they have anything, I'm sure they'll be happy to send it to you.

If they don't have any printed material, see if you can get an agent to come by and conduct a class with questions and answers for you. These agencies often include education as part of their mission.  I'm sure every agency in America would be happy to help you to help them.

## Enforcement Action Beyond Minor Stings

I would be doing you a disservice if I left you with the impression that minor stings are the only ways you can run into trouble if you are not carding people properly.  Law enforcement can investigate, cite, prosecute and punish you in other ways if you are not exercising the proper caution and due diligence when it comes to proper carding.

Law enforcement does not need a minor to present an ID or to conduct a minor sting.  Law enforcement who is responsible for overseeing regulated activities like alcohol and marijuana sales can just walk into your business and observe.  They can and will watch what your systems and procedures are and will evaluate them then and there.  If they find them lacking, they may identify themselves and conduct an investigation then and there.

I will give you an example.

Imagine that an alcohol enforcement agent is in your bar and is observing, but has not identified themselves to the employees.

She sees a group of young people come into the bar, order drinks and get served.  No one is carded during this process.

At this point she, most likely, has the legal authority to go up to the group, identify herself and card them as the bartender should have done. If any of them are underage, the bartender could be cited. If there are laws in place that require carding below a minimum age, the bartender can also be cited, even if everyone is of age.

All of this could have been avoided if the bartender had done their job and done it well to begin with.

I will give you another example.

Imagine a group of college kids run afoul of campus security after a night at your bar. Campus security is not law enforcement. However, they make a complaint to law enforcement reporting that minors were served in your bar on a specific date and time.

Law enforcement can choose to launch an investigation. This can involve review of security cameras and recordings. Many businesses have cameras that document everything that goes on in an age restricted environment for liability purposes. If those recordings, which are often required to be made available to law enforcement, show you performing less than your legally required duty to carding; you can be cited.

This can also be true in the event that a minor is caught drunk driving, or worse, is involved in an accident. If this happens, police will normally ask then where they were drinking. That information will then be forwarded to the agency responsible for enforcing regulation. Then, just like before, an investigation can result, recordings can be reviewed and citations issued.

We live in a surveillance society. The low cost of powerful and reliable recording devices makes it very likely you are being recorded every time you are involved in a controlled, regulated activity like bartending or selling marijuana.

Those recordings become a record of how you conducted yourself and whether you complied with the law. I don't say this to scare you, just to encourage you to do a thorough and professional job that always complies with the law.

I have had experiences with all three of the examples I presented here. I have seen people fired and people fined and prosecuted resulting from the review of recordings. It can and does happen and should encourage you to comply with the law 100% of the time.

## Conclusion

Before you can spot fake IDs, you need to build a solid foundation of technique to inspect IDs. You need to know what to look for, what features are present on IDs and what they tell you. You need to card people following a methodical, reflexive procedure that follows the same sequence each and every time.

You have learned everything you need to know to make that a reality in this chapter. It is up to you to take this information and to make it part of your normal work routine and then turn it into habit.

Once you do, you will be much more likely and able to use what you learn in the next chapter to effectively spot fake IDs.

## Part 3: Spotting Fake IDs

In this part of the book we will be exploring fake IDs. We will discuss the world of modern fake IDs and what to look for to help you spot fake IDs. We will discuss a variety of strategies to flush out and expose people offering your employees fake IDs.

Lastly, we will be discussing what you should do and what you should empower your employees to do in the event that they run into a suspected fake ID situation.

A lot of the hard work in catching fake IDs is just paying attention to small details that become obvious once you are aware of them.

**Defining the fake ID problem.**

To begin, let's talk about who sells modern fake IDs and where they come from.

When I first entered the world of bars and restaurants, the fake IDs we encountered were either modified IDs or IDs that belonged to another person. People would change a date, or maybe a picture. They might use an older sibling's ID that they stole over the holidays.

At the time, Hollywood loved to make it seem like everyone bought a brand new, counterfeit IDs from windowless white vans. These vans were parked across the street from every high school and college dorm in America. At the time, that was a bit of a romantic fiction, but with the advent of low cost, sophisticated computers and printers, along with the internet and global communications and shipping, it has become a bit of a reality.

You can go online, right now as you read this and type in "buy a fake ID" to any search engine in the world and you will be provided with more offers than you know what to do with. They will be from every state and territory in America and many countries around the world. They will be high quality and very well done. They will scan and depict your picture in a seamless manner that will fool many bartenders, bouncers and shop clerks.

Some of these companies and websites even offer volume discounts to enterprising college freshmen who solicit and enlist their fellow classmates. It's unbridled, illegal capitalism.

You pay for your ID over the internet with a credit card, send them a picture after you make your selection and your new, fake ID will arrive in the mail. Easy as pie.

Who is selling these IDs?

As a general rule, it's organized and sophisticated criminal networks who are technologically savvy. I won't name any one country. The shops are portable and have been known to move frequently to stay one step ahead of law enforcement. We live in a global economy and these networks that sell fake IDs are some of the most global businesses out there.

Why are these available?

Frankly, because it's a low priority issue. Although this is a problem and does generate money for criminal networks, it doesn't cause the damage or perceived harm that drug trafficking, terrorism and weapons sales do. Frankly, it's more akin to knock off Italian designer brands and high end, counterfeit consumer electronics. Highly profitable, but lower attention and lower risk.

The fact is that this problem will probably grow worse before it grows better. Because of this, it will probably be a problem and a risk that you and your employees will have to manage for some time to come.

As with everything else in this book you will manage it with ongoing training. Like I said in the introduction, these IDs can be spotted fairly easily if you know what to look for and learn to pay attention to details that many carding professionals will overlook.

## Which IDs are likely to be fake?

You can make your job of spotting fake IDs much easier if you can reduce the total number of IDs that you need to be suspicious of. Looking an ID over to try and determine if it's a fake takes a bit longer to do. It's generally impractical to do this for every ID you are presented with.

If you can reduce the number of IDs that merit extra scrutiny, you can direct your attention more to where it needs to be for your particular situation and business. Here are a few thoughts and ideas that may help you to reduce that number.

## Passports

It's a lot easier to order some fake IDs than it is to order others.

Generally speaking, the fake IDs that you are likely to encounter are national or state issued IDs. Examples of these would be an EU National ID card or a driver's license from Maryland.

Generally speaking, it's very hard to get a counterfeit passport. For immigration, citizenship and anti-terrorism reasons, global law enforcement takes this issue much more seriously. Additionally, a passport is a much more complicated and security enhanced document. Even if they were available as easily as national and state IDs, they would be prohibitively expensive.

As a general rule, this cost will make it unlikely, although not impossible that you will encounter many fake passports.

## Non-local IDs

The vast majority of fake IDs I have encountered in my career have been non-local IDs. These generally should prompt extra scrutiny.

If you stop and think about this for a few minutes, you'll understand why this is the case.

People who check IDs as part of their work see a lot of IDs. A bartender, liquor store clerk, casino employee or budtender will look at a lot of IDs in a normal day. For most, the majority of IDs will be local. If they live in California, a budtender will see a lot of California IDs. A Florida bartender will be very familiar with the Florida driver's license.

As part of the plan to get past an ID check, it has been my experience that many underage people will try to use a non-local ID. That Florida bartender will have less experience with Montana driver's license. That California budtender will have much less experience with a driver's license from Connecticut.

This unfamiliarity raises the chances that they won't notice mistakes or inconsistencies. They may not be familiar with the city that is printed on the ID, let alone the address. They may be rushed or impatient and just assume the ID is valid rather than admitting that they don't know or are unsure of something. That kind of bluff can work.

This raises the chances of success for the underage person and makes non-local IDs more desirable and worthy of that extra attention.

Whenever you get a non-local ID, take a few extra seconds to take note of it and study it. With the techniques that will follow in this book you can significantly raise the chances of identifying a fake and eliminating a compliance risk.

**Old ID Version**

In the United States each state issues a unique driver's license and ID card. There is no national ID card or standard. In addition to this, many of the states will have multiple versions of driver's licenses and IDs circulating. This is usually because an old version is being or has been retired and is or has been replaced by a new version.

However, a new version does not mean that everyone who has the old version has to get the new one. The effect of this is that there may be a current and an "old" version of every ID from every state in America.

This is further complicated by the fact that this is an ongoing process that repeats every few years.

All of this adds up to a lot of valid ID formats circulating around all at once. It is very likely that you will encounter an old version of an ID that has not expired quickly once you begin checking lots of IDs.

These IDs are almost always worthy of extra attention.

Why?

ID issuing authorities and forgers who make fake IDs are in a constant battle. Issuers try to retire designs and add security features before forgers can produce fake IDs based on these designs. Forgers constantly try to win the race and produce a good forgery before the issuer comes out with a new, security enhanced ID.

Issuers change their designs frequently to create a moving target, but they don't always win the race. Sometimes, even when a new version comes out, forgers will offer the old one because these designs are still in circulation, can pass a basic inspection, and people will pay for them.

As a rule with the non-local IDs, I would encourage you to always pay extra attention to older versions of IDs. Just like non-local IDs, with the extra techniques you will soon learn, you can significantly reduce the risk that these IDs will get past you undetected.

To prepare for this challenge, I would again recommend that you spend time studying a current guide to IDs. Study the pictures of versions in circulation. Learn which ones are the new ones and which designs have been retired, but are still in circulation. They are prime candidates to be fake IDs.

This is not an exhaustive list of the IDs that can and are faked, but it is a list of ID types that I have personally seen faked many times. They are a list that deserves extra screening and attention to detail.

This is just one line of defense to help you catch fake IDs and eliminate this problem in your business and professional life. In the remainder of this section, we will be adding others. No one is sufficient on its own, but taken together, they will give you a strong defense and a good toolbox to catch fake IDs.

**What information is being faked?**

It can be very helpful to know what ID is being faked on a fake ID. This can help you to catch the person trying to pass the ID in lies and holes in their knowledge.

You might think that with a fake ID, they are just changing the year on the birthday. This, in my experience, is not the case.

Usually most of the information on an ID is going to be fake with the exception of the name of the person and maybe the address. We will talk more about addresses later.

That means the address, their birthday, the year they first got a driver's license, their zip code, and their state are all false.

Why is this helpful?

Since most of the information on the ID will be false or borrowed from a real person, it creates a lot of lies that a person using the ID illegally has to keep straight. That's especially hard when they're nervous about passing off a fake ID. That creates a lot of chances for you to trip the person up and to expose the ID as fake. It also creates a lot of chances for the forgers who made the ID to make mistakes as well.

All of these can be used to expose a fake ID.

**Contextual Screening - Which one doesn't belong?**

Who is using a fake ID?

The person is young, obviously, they are under 18 or 21 depending on the regulated activity. That's easy.

Why did they get a fake ID?

People who get fake IDs do so to go out with friends and to do things socially. I'm sure it happens, but the vast majority of people who get fake IDs do not do so to go out by themselves and read a book in a booth at a local bar.

They get fake IDs so they can go out as a group on Fridays and Saturdays to spend time with friends, meet people to date, and make memories.

That information is useful to someone trying to spot fake IDs because you can intuit that you need to watch people in large groups and social gatherings much more closely.

If a large group of young people comes into your business and you are going to card them, start paying close attention to the group as quickly as possible. Study them.

Do they all look the same age?

Is anyone hanging at the back of the group and seems more reluctant? Maybe more nervous?

As you start to card them, pay attention to the dates of their birthdays.

Is everyone born in the same year?

I have caught many fake IDs in this situation.

For some reason people who buy fake IDs often do so with a birthdate that is noticeably out of line with their peers. Everyone in a group might have been born in 1997 and then just one of them will have an ID that says 1995.

It's possible that they just happen to have an older friend, but it's certainly worth extra suspicion. Often on closer inspection these outliers turn out to be fake.

Whenever you're looking at a group of IDs, try and put them into context and understand how they relate to each other. Whenever you have one or two that are out of place and just make less sense, take some extra time and take a closer look at that ID. It's very possible that it's a fake.

## Watch Their Body Language

If you've ever played poker you will know that people have tells. A tell is some minute physical twitch or motion or fidgeting that can tell you a lot about the other player.

Someone trying to pass off a fake ID will have tells too. If they're in a large group they may be the one hanging back. They're nervous about trying out their fake ID for the first time.

They might avoid eye contact. People who are lying often do.

Watch them when they take their ID out of their wallet. Are they fidgeting? Is the motion of their hand normal? Relaxed? Are they shaking?

I have seen all of these behaviors up close many times. It's understandable. They're committing a crime and they're nervous they're going to get caught. They're nervous of legal and social penalties that can be imposed on them. They're nervous they'll make a mistake and their friends will make fun of them. Trust me. Someone passing off a fake ID for the first time will be thinking about getting arrested and having their future ruined.

What should you do in this case?

Frankly, make it worse for them.

When I have encountered this situation and want to test things a little, I'll usually say something like:

- Why are you so nervous?

- You seem really nervous?
- Something bothering you? Your hands are shaking.

As you might imagine, this does not help people who are already nervous to relax. Frankly, it is more likely to make them panic. I have literally seen people run out of a bar after I have said this to them without ever giving me their ID.

Now, this is not a normal reaction for a normal person conducting normal, legal business. I assumed his ID was fake and he had no business in my bar.

Watch how people behave when you card them. It's a powerful screening tool. If you pay attention to small details, you can quickly pick up when something is not right and can use that to your advantage.

## Check The ID As You Normally Would

When I'm suspicious of an ID, I will check it using the normal process that I described in the previous section. This is the first thing that I will do.

Making this the first step in a fake ID investigation will also keep you from getting distracted and skipping these essential steps. It will also reinforce it as a good professional habit.

## Check The Issue Date

After I verify that a suspicious ID would be valid for entry, if real, I check the issue date.

As a reminder, the issue date is the day that the ID was supposedly printed by the ID issuer like the DMV.

Why do I do this?

There are two tripwires in this date that can be used to determine that an ID is fake.

The first tripwire is how old the ID is.

I want you to imagine that an ID has an issue date that says it is three years old. Fake IDs that are only a few weeks old will often have dates like this.

When you get a real ID, you put it in your purse or wallet. You take it out and put it back for lots of different reasons. You show it at the bank, to get on a plane or to buy beer. All of that in and out and daily life takes a toll on the ID. Go get yours right now and look at it. You will see fine scratches and wear and tear. That's just normal.

Fake IDs don't live the same life. They're only taken out for special occasions. A lot of people won't carry them day to day. That means they live a sheltered life free from wear and tear.

When you see a fake ID and you look for those scratches and wear and tear, it will often be completely absent. This is always a huge red flag for me.

To look for these, shine a light on the ID and look at the protective film that covers the ID. What does it tell you? Has this ID been well used? If it hasn't been worn or well used and is still shiny, give it extra scrutiny or consider moving on to one of the other steps we will talk about shortly.

What is the other tripwire in the issue date?

The other tripwire applies to old versions of an ID that are presented to you. When an ID issuer phases out an ID, they will announce a retirement date. This is the date, after which, only the new format will be issued.

If you have an old ID with an issue date after the retirement date, you have a very suspicious ID and you should probably refuse service.

Where can you find the retirement dates?

It's in your ID guide which you keep close when checking IDs. Flip to the state in question and check and then compare the info in the book with the ID. Don't be afraid to take your time and do this right.

While it's conceivable the person in front of you has an ID that was printed after the retirement date, using a format that was retired, it is highly unlikely and suspicious. Any time I have run into this situation, I have just politely declined service. Remember, it's always better to be safe rather than sorry. This is doubly true when the consequences are large fines and criminal prosecution.

## UV Ink Errors and Inconsistencies

I would encourage you to get in the habit of shining a UV flashlight on every ID you examine. It should just be part of the process. Many, if not all of the IDs out there, will have UV features that will appear at this point.

I have caught many fake IDs by examining the UV features.

It's not at all uncommon to see UV feature errors on fake IDs. I have seen the wrong part of the ID light up under the ultraviolet light. I have seen the wrong state seal on an ID. I have seen UV features on IDs that aren't supposed to have one.

How do you check the features?

You refer back to your reference guide. In each reference guide you will find a section that shows all the current UV features for all the IDs that have them. Make it a part of your professional development to study them. Look the section over when you have downtime. It's important work that only helps the business. Studying an ID guide is never wasted time.

If you have an ID that has a UV feature that you are unfamiliar with, take that extra minute to look it up and study it right then and there. I did this once and the young woman just ran right out the door and left me holding the ID. After studying it carefully, I knew it was fake because the UV features were wrong.

Forgers don't just make mistakes. They're sloppy too.

The printers who make IDs for issuing authorities like states and governments are very precise. They should be. Issuers, like states, are not tolerant of errors where these lucrative contracts are concerned.

Forgers are nowhere near as exact. One example of sloppiness I have seen repeated over and over is the UV features. Often you will see drips of UV ink where they shouldn't be any. Look carefully while your flashlight is on.

Personally, when I saw these drips, I would decline service because the IDs are suspect. I might not have been able to prove they were fake in a court of law, but the drips are more than enough to raise my suspicion beyond a comfortable level.

**Heuristic Challenges**

Let's talk about the word heuristic. What does it mean?

It simply means a practical, not perfect solution to a problem that someone can carry out quickly and by themselves.

When you're trying to spot a fake ID, it would be really nice to have a quick simple test that you can use to help you. That's where the heuristic challenge comes in. It's exactly the type of test you need. They are quick, flexible and can usually give you a good gut feeling on whether an ID is legitimate or not.

A heuristic challenge is just a question or series of questions that you can ask a person who has a possibly fake ID to try and trip them up and possibly reveal their lie. An example might help.

Imagine you live in Connecticut. A man walks into your bar with an ID from Louisiana. You think it's fake. He's probably memorized every bit of information on that ID. He will know the address and the birth date (let's say 1993) and all of that.

He might very well be from Louisiana. So test him.

Ask him to name the capital of Louisiana.

Ask him to name two states that border Louisiana.

Ask him the highway that runs through the capital of Louisiana.

Ask him the governor of Louisiana.

These are all heuristic challenges and how he answers will help you decide if he is probably being honest or not. If he names the capital immediately. He might be telling the truth. If he says New Orleans (it's Baton Rouge) quickly like he believes it, maybe he's just bad at geography.

The chances are low that someone with a fake ID has memorized all of this information. If you aren't from Louisiana, you might not know which states border it. If you are from there, you will most likely know it reflexively.

You don't even have to know the right answer to the question. You are deciding what is most likely and what to do based on **HOW** they answer, not on **WHAT** they answer. You can ask anything you want. I have no idea what states border Kansas. However, I have asked and judged answers to that question many times.

So, ask a question.

Then you have to decide what to do next. If his answer is natural, quick and effortless, he might be telling the truth. If he gets it wrong, or has to think really hard, starts fidgeting or looks nervous, or starts telling you a long, unlikely story, you should get much more suspicious.

It's important that you need to understand that this is not a black and white test. You will have to observe people when they answer and use your judgement.

It's entirely possible someone with a fake ID may learn everything about their fake ID and they state they claim issued it. That's OK. We have something for that - math.

Another favorite technique I used to trip people up with fake IDs was to ask how old they were in a certain year. For example:

"How old were you in 2005?"

If their ID says they were born in 1993, then they should answer 12. A lot of the time, they don't.

Instead, they try to do math in their head while keeping a poker face which never works. People will look up or get a confused, panicked look on their face. A lot of the time because they are nervous and stressed out, they will respond with their actual age in that year. I had one person just blurt out "10" when I was looking for "12".

They failed that heuristic challenge.

The nice thing about math oriented challenges is you can tailor them to the situation and ask multiple ones in a row. No one can prepare for that by studying a map. After two or three questions, people with fake IDs will usually get tripped up and tip their hand.

Not everyone fails a heuristic challenge. Sometimes, the challenge completely satisfies and convinces you. I didn't choose Louisiana by mistake. Once I had a man come in with a Louisiana ID. For some reason I wasn't convinced of its authenticity.

I asked him to name the state capital. He answered without even thinking. Then, he went on to express his support for a famous Louisiana college football team. Then, without even asking, he pulled his underwear up just a bit so I could also see that they too supported the same football team.

Needless to say, I was convinced at that point. Any suspicions I had had melted away as he demonstrated his comfort with and knowledge of Louisiana. He went on to become a regular face in that bar.

As you're carding, lean on the heuristic challenge anytime you are uncertain or suspicious of someone's ID. It's a powerful tool that can eliminate much of the fake ID problem in your business if used consistently and publicly.

Eventually word will get around that you're careful about fake IDs and they'll just go elsewhere.

**Go In The Back**

One reason that I trained you to have them take the ID out of their wallet and hand it to you was so you could touch and feel it.

Another reason was so you control the ID for a minute. They do the same thing at a customs counter when you cross international borders. This gives you a tremendously useful tool to catch fake IDs.

You just go in the back somewhere.

You just go somewhere out of sight for a minute or two and see how the person who presented the suspicious ID reacts. Someone who just handed you a fake ID, which is proof of a crime, will get very, very nervous.

They don't know what you're doing or if you're calling the police. Their heart is pounding and their palms are sweating. More than once, people have just run out the front door and left me with their fake ID.

There are all sorts of ways to excuse yourself. Say you have to ask your manager about a feature on the ID. Say you have to check something. Just say "Excuse me for a moment." and walk away. Let their nervous imagination decide what you're doing.

Someone with a real, legitimate ID will have no problem waiting a moment. They've got nothing to worry about. For someone trying to pass a fake, every minute will be torture and many of them will not be able to stand it.

Don't be gone too long. Limit it to a few minutes and make use of the time. Study the ID closely. It's not a bad idea to keep a copy of the ID checking guide in the back for quick reference in situations like this.

**Get Out Your Book And Make A Show Of It**

Another heuristic challenge I have been known to use involves your ID checking guide. If I suspect an ID, I will get the book out and check the ID against the information in the book. The only thing is, I won't go in the back to do it. I will do it right there in front of the person I am suspicious of. I'll take an extra minute, be through and I'll see what they do.

I've had people get nervous, decide to leave and ask for their ID back. As far as I'm concerned that is a failed test. When they decide to leave, I would generally give them their ID back and let them go on their way.

Sometimes, people would rush me or tell me I didn't need to check anything. Those were failed tests too.

Like with any heuristic challenge, it will be up to you and your instincts whether or not someone passed. You are the person whose licenses and livelihood are on the line. It will be your call whether to take the risk and accept an ID or not.

**Using Online Maps**

A few years back I stumbled on a newer technique to challenge fake IDs. It involves the address on the IDs.

What I noticed were odd addresses that didn't match the states the IDs were from. For example "123 Redondo Beach Lane" on an ID from Missouri. Redondo Beach is a famous city in California. There isn't a Redondo Beach in Missouri. In fact, there aren't really beaches in Missouri.

I got suspicious and I whipped out my phone and I did a quick map search using the ID in my hand and sure enough, no address. Google was confused!  It was a smoking gun as far as I was concerned.  When I went back, I told the kid there wasn't an address like that and that I thought it was best I call the cops to sort it all out.

He immediately left.  He didn't argue or anything.  That was a pretty good validation that the ID was fake.  At my discretion, if an ID has an address I can't validate, usually I'm going to decline service.

This is a good test and a lot of the fake IDs that are in my collection have bad addresses on them.  If you look them up, no results come up.

It might be that the house is new and Google doesn't know about it yet.  It happens.  If they pull out a bunch of secondary IDs to back up the first one and they all have the same address, hear them out.  If they have nothing else with that address on it, it should raise an eyebrow.

It's up to you to decide how to use this and what to do with the results.  You can do it in the back.  You can do it in front of the person and then ask them to explain why the internet is not aware that their house exists.  That's a pretty big oversight in today's interconnected world.

I would think of this test as a way to validate suspicions that have already been aroused by other anomalies.  You most likely don't have the time to check every ID that comes in.  There are privacy concerns as well.  People don't like to have their data collected left and right.  However, if you are already suspicious this can be a very good check to confirm those suspicions.

If the internet does have their address listed, this also gives you extra tools for heuristic challenges.  Pull up an image of the house.  Look at it.  Ask them to describe it.  Ask them what color it is and see how they react.

## What To Do With A Suspicious ID

If you have learned anything from this book I hope it would be that spotting fake IDs is not usually a black and white issue. Instead it is a world of gray that is made up mostly of hunches, observations, gut feelings and suspicions.

That being said, if you are carding sooner or later, you will run into an ID you just don't trust. Then what do you do?

That question has a simple answer. You decline service. You don't let them in your bar or shop. You don't sell them marijuana. You don't serve them alcohol.

That's it. You should be polite. You should be professional. You just don't offer them products or services for which they have not offered sufficient proof of age.

<u>If you remember nothing else from this book, remember that one.</u>

How do you refuse service?

The answer to that question is harder.

There are wrong ways to do it and there are right ways to do it. You can refuse service unprofessionally and you can refuse service professionally. I'm going to teach you how to do it professionally.

### Keep Things Calm

First things first, stay calm. You are not holding a live hand grenade. Most likely, you are holding some nineteen year old college kid's fake ID. It won't hurt you, especially now that you know it's fake.

Refusing service can be a delicate situation though. People can get aggravated when they are called out and embarrassed. You want to avoid that.

If you can, get them alone, away from a group they may have come in with. This will allow them to save their pride. It will also cut down on peer support. When you separate someone from a group, in my experience, they become much more compliant, reasonable and easier to manage.

If you can't get them away from a group, don't yell, don't swear or insult them. I have seen all of that done and it never helps the situation. Your job is to protect your license and get them out the door with the minimum of trouble. When you shout insults at people in front of their friends, you only create a headache for yourself.

Talk calmly, slowly and at your normal volume. Plus, remember to breathe.

## Keep The ID In Your Hands

If you follow the instructions in this book, you will be holding the ID in question when you decide it is fake. Good!

Try to hold onto it when you are declining service.

This gives you some leverage. A person who knows you have a picture of them will behave better. This also encourages them to cooperate. If they behave badly they may not get their ID back. If they behave badly, that ID which may be fake, might find its way to the police or college authorities.

You don't say any of this though. You just hold the ID and let them think these things as you talk to them in a calm, normal, respectful way.

## Politely Declining Service

When I'm refusing service because I believe an ID is fake, as opposed to an expired or punched ID, I have a script I use. Usually I will say something like:

**"I'm pretty sure this is a fake ID. I'm not going to take it tonight, but I'm not going to allow you into the bar."**

There are three parts to this phrase and I think it's worth looking at all of them.

First, you are telling them that you know it's fake, or at least are deeply suspicious. It's important to make this clear right away. If it's fake, their heart will be beating faster and they will know that the cat's out of the bag.

Next, you tell them that you will not confiscate the ID **"TONGIHT".** That leaves open the threat that if you see it again, you might. It makes someone a lot less likely to bring the ID back. A big part of solving the fake ID problem is getting them to know that you are vigilant and alert. This sentence encourages them to take their fake ID business elsewhere.

Lastly, you tell them that you will not be allowing them to access your services in a clear, concise way.

You can use this script all you want. You can change it however you want too. Reword it and make it your own. I would, however, advise you to have a script in your head. Say it the same way every time. This will make it habit and reflexive. You will know what to do and what to say and this will help you stay calm and professional.

Your script is an essential tool just like your flashlight and heuristic challenges are.

**Don't Argue**

A lot of the time, when you tell someone that you will not accept their ID, they will want to argue the point with you. I would always advise against creating a situation where it appears that the matter is up for discussion.

What I would encourage you to do is be transparent in your reason why you are refusing to accept the ID.

In the event that the ID is expired, tell them that and explain that the house policy or the law is to not accept expired IDs. If you believe that the ID is fake, tell them that in a straightforward manner.

I would say something like:

**"In my professional judgement, I do not feel comfortable accepting this ID. I believe it may be fake and therefore, I can't accept it."**

This is the point, where sadly, some people feel that they might be able to convince you that you're wrong.

If you're the final decision maker, such as a manager, you can add something like:

**"I'm sorry, that's going to have to be my final decision on the matter."**

If you're not the final decisions maker, this is where you would escalate the situation and loop your manager in.

**Follow The Chain Of Command**

If you're not the final authority in the establishment you work in, it's always a good idea to loop in your boss as soon as possible when refusing service. Picking up where we left off in the last section, you could say something like:

**"In my professional judgement, I do not feel comfortable accepting this ID. I believe it may be fake and therefore, I can't accept it. That's going to have to be my final decision on the matter, but if you'd like, I can grab my manager for you to talk to."**

This is a good script when a situation is escalating. It gives you some space to step away and grab the manager. It also gets you out of the situation and back to doing your job and making money. Lastly, it puts the onus of managing a delicate customer service situation on the manager, who should be backing you up in these situations.

As a rule, whenever I work in a job that requires carding, and there is a service refusal situation, I will loop a manager in as soon as possible. Sometimes this means when a situation is still in progress and they want to argue with my decisions. Sometimes it means just after a situation has ended if the kids took their fake ID and left without an issue.

Either way, good communication is key to having your manager's trust and a good working relationship. Additionally, the manager's job is to support you in operations. Alerting them when you need that support will make your job easier too.

**Stand Firm**

Some people are going to want to argue the point and try and convince you that you are wrong. A lot of them will try and get you to set aside your own judgement and bluff their way through. Don't let them. If you've read this book and your intuition is telling you something isn't right, then refuse service. It's best to protect your license and your business if you're in doubt.

Once you've made a call stick with it. Don't let a customer bluff or bully you into ignoring your intuition.

I have done that once or twice in a hospitality career that spans decades. I can also tell you with certainty I have come to regret it almost every time. Don't be afraid to stand firm.

**Threaten To Call The Police**

I have had plenty of young people with fake IDs try to bluff their way through me once I have caught them with a fake ID. I would usually say something like:

**"We can just call the police and let them sort it out if you'd like."**

Usually, this is where they would decide to fold. They'd leave and that'd be that. Sometimes, however, somebody might insist that "WE" do in fact call the police to verify.

What do you do then?

I would always tell them that they are welcome to call the police if they like and that they could wait outside for them to arrive. I would then politely ask them to go wait outside of the bar or restaurant while they waited.

Almost without exception the person with the questionable ID would get tired of waiting (police as a whole are in no hurry to come verify an ID at a bar) and would move along. Once they're outside and they know they're staying outside, more often than not, they rethink their plan and decide to go home.

Either way, at that point, from your perspective, the problem is solved.

## Documenting The Interaction

No matter how a situation with a suspicious ID turns out, I would encourage you to document it. This helps with liability and it also helps you to remember events long after they have happened. You never know when it can be useful. Memories fade and you don't want to rely on your recollection when talking to law enforcement.

Several times in my career, I have had to rely on documentation and I've had to present it to law enforcement. In each case it turned out fine because I had a dated, documented statement before they asked for it.

It could be that your establishment has a log for everyone to write in. This is a common practice in many businesses. If there is one, use it and make sure you document every noteworthy event. If you forget to write things down one day, make sure you correct that ASAP.

If your business does not have a log policy, talking to your manager about starting one might be a good idea. Logs and documentation protect everyone including the manager and the business.

Another way you can document an event is with an email. Send an email to yourself. Write a subject line that you will remember like "May 5th 2018 - Fake ID Incident". That way you can find it later if someone asks for it.

The nice thing about emailing yourself is that it is timestamped. You can prove when you wrote it and this can be useful in legal settings or investigations.

If your bar does have a log, there is nothing that says you can't send yourself an email too. Logs have been known to get lost and the double layer of documentation will be handy if you ever need it. I promise!

## Confiscating Suspicious IDs

When we talked about heuristic challenges and what those are, I explained that they are simple tests that allow you to make a gut level judgement quickly. They are very useful in fast paced environments and usually you will be correct.

However, it would be silly to assume that we are 100% right 100% of the time. The truth is from time to time, you are going to make a bad call. It happens, get used to it now and accept it. However, making no call is worse than making a bad call.

I 'm not telling you to ignore your intuition or even to be open to discussing your ID related decisions. I'm just telling you to accept that you may be wrong from time to time.

I'm using this idea as a segue into the concept of taking suspicious IDs.

Frankly, I'm against taking IDs from people because there's a real possibility you might be wrong.

What happens when you take someone's ID? They get angry. They get confrontational. They get aggressive. All of those are bad in a business environment. It might create a disturbance or even an altercation. Those make your establishment look bad. They alarm other paying customers. They take your time away from paying activities to non-paying activities.

Frankly, in my opinion, taking IDs is bad for business.

What happens if you take someone's **REAL** ID by mistake?

Well, you can bet that they'll be mad. You can bet that they'll tell everyone and anyone they know. In today's social media environment, that can become a big number.

You'll lose them as a customer and they may take some of their friends with them.

Again, in my opinion, taking IDs is bad for business.

At this point, you might be thinking by refusing to serve someone, you will lose their business anyway.

That's not necessarily true.

I have certainly turned away people with fake IDs who eventually came back with their real ones when they had turned 21. They had an "all's fair in love and war" attitude about it. Some of them even became pretty good customers and one or two became good friends.

What if you turn someone away who gives you their real ID?

That can be managed too. If someone argues with me and seems pretty sincere that their ID is real, although I think it's fake, I will often make them an offer. I will say something like:

**"Look, I'm just looking out for my business here. I'll tell you what. Bring me your passport so I can be sure and I'll buy you a beer."**

This is an olive branch that can help defuse those situations where you're just not quite sure. I have made this offer plenty of times. Most of the time the customer in question hasn't come back. That's when I knew I was right. However, a few of them have come back and they brought their passports. They matched the ID I had been suspicious about. That's when I knew I wasn't 100% right 100% of the time.

When that happened, I always honored our deal and the customer was usually satisfied. Sometime, I'd even make a new friend out of the deal because I had handled it professionally and honestly with them.

Any customer service business is a dynamic business and you will often have to think on your feet and improvise solutions to problems. That is still true when it comes to IDs and carding people. While I would never advise you ignore carding regulations or ignore your gut, I would advise that you be nice, professional and as helpful as you can be.

Now, you might also be thinking that if you leave fake IDs in circulation, you're part of the problem and they might come back where you work.

I have a couple of thoughts on that too.

First, it's not your job to confiscate fake IDs. Unless the law requires you to, again, I would recommend you do not. The risk is high for an altercation or taking someone's real ID by mistake. However, that doesn't mean you can't vaguely threaten to take their ID.

If I feel the need to dissuade people from brining a fake ID where I work, I will often say something like:

**"I'm not going to take your fake ID tonight, but if you bring it back here, I might not be so nice."**

Most of the people I have said this to become wide eyed and alarmed and I never see the fake ID again. They don't know that I really hate the idea of confiscating an ID. It's another bluff, but it deals with most of the problem without any confrontation or trouble. Most of the time they quietly leave.

But what if they come back when one of your coworkers is working who isn't as thorough as you?

I have an answer for that too. Offer your coworkers help with spotting fake IDs.. Share your insight with them. Teach them if they ask or accept your offer. A chain is only as strong as its weakest link. After reading this book you can certainly help them to improve their carding.

If you don't want to do the work, let me! Tell them about this book! It's a shameless plug, but if this book helped you, can help them too!

You can also ask your manager for more training. Like I said before, regulating authorities will often come and teach classes. Ask them to make a call or even go so far as to volunteer to do it yourself.

If you're the manager, build a training program. Put policies and systems in place so your employees know what to do before a situation comes up. Assure them of your support and willingness to help. Encourage them to ask questions and share knowledge. Start using a log and make it available to everyone. This will help your employees know what's going on and will help to build a strong, effective, profitable team.

**What To Do With Fakes In Your Possession**

I have been clear on how I feel about taking IDs, but not everyone is going to listen to me. Additionally, I've talked several times of people running out of my restaurant and leaving me holding their fake ID. It absolutely happens.

The fact is that if you work in a business that cards people, you may wind up with some fake IDs in your possession from time to time.

What do you do with them?

First, they are great teaching aids! Figure out how to prove they're fake and show everyone on staff. Make sure they understand. As we talked about earlier, when you find one fake, you will often find others of the same type.

Should I display them as a warning?

I don't like to display them. This can expose people's private information and embarrass them. This is bad from a customer service point of view, in my opinion. I've known places that do it, but frankly it's not my style and I would recommend against it.

How do I get rid of fake IDs?

Most law enforcement agencies will take fake IDs off your hands. They use them as teaching aids too and can also use them to help reduce the fake ID problem. I would encourage you to give any fake IDs that come your way, once your team is educated on them, to law enforcement. This will also show to them that you are vigilant and are doing your part!

## Conclusion

In this book we have covered a lot of ground. You've learned a lot about carding and how to do it properly, professionally, and effectively. You have the tools you need at this point, but it's up to you to use them. It's up to you to adopt the habits and techniques you learned in this book. It's up to you to make them part of every workday. It's up to you to cultivate new habits. It's up to you to drive your workplace culture to a better place.

I have confidence, if you have read this book and digested its contents, you can do exactly that. You can make your workplace safer and more responsible. You've got this!

Thomas Morrell
-Uniform23 Training

www.ingramcontent.com/pod-product-compliance
Lightning Source LLC
Chambersburg PA
CBHW070941210326
41520CB00021B/6996